Birmingham: It's Not Shit

50 Things That Delight About Brum

www.paradisecircus.com

First published by Paradise Circus in 2021.

Copyright © Paradise Circus 2021.

Set in Baskerville, because anything else feels like treason.

The authors assert the moral right to be identified as the authors of this work, whatever that means.

A catalogue record for this book is available from the British Library. A Library of Birmingham catalogue is available if you have a long enough ladder.

ISBN 978-1-80068-399-0

All rights reserved. No part of this publication may be reproduced, stored in a retrieval system, or transmitted, in any form or by any means, electronic, mechanical, photocopying, recording or otherwise, without the prior written permission of the publishers.

"I travel by train to New Street Station, then walk the length of Lichfield Road towards The Junction. And with each step I feel closer and closer to the very heart of something that can never be defined." Bill Drummond, 9 November 2021

Birmingham: It's Not Shit

50 Things That Delight About Brum

Foreword by Adrian Chiles

A few years ago I was filming something in Birmingham. Being a generous sort I took the crew to lunch, at a Pizza Hut in Selly Oak. On the glass above the salad bar there was taped a notice which read, PLEASE DON'T COUGH OR SNEEZE ON THE FOOD.

There was something very Birmingham about that, and not in a bad way. It's a bit disgusting, obviously, and no one bothered with the salad that lunchtime, but it's direct and it's funny. And relating the story — as I have done countless times — with some twisted kind of pride, well, that's very Birmingham too.

It took a bloke from Surrey to help me understand what it is I love so much about my own home town. He was called Rajesh and had been based in the city for a couple of years as the BBC's Midlands Correspondent when I met him.

"What I really like about Birmingham," he said, "Is that the people don't big themselves or the city up. And they're the richer for it."

I'd never thought about it like that before. I felt great pride surging through my veins as I accepted his compliment most humbly on behalf of all Brummies. And soon afterwards I was delighted to find that the same idea was available in website form. www.birminghamitsnotshit.co.uk is the greatest URL in the history of the internet. The name conveyed so much with such concision that it didn't matter if the content was any good or not (it was).

Yes, we sit proudly at the bottom of the league table of civic self-regard and long may it stay that way. I enjoy watching the battle for the top spot in this league of self-love, even though there are only ever two contenders for the title: Manchester and Yorkshire have been tussling over it for years. "Manchester, the second city? Nah, that's London," they say. Yawn. "Yorkshire: God's own.." Yeah, whatever.

Why do they think it's a good idea to speak like this about themselves? If a bloke walks into a bar and stands around telling anyone who'll listen how great he is, everyone in there will think he's a) insecure and b) a twat. Banging on about your city or county has exactly the same effect.

We've never done it, don't do it, and never will. As such we're becoming a rare species indeed, for this is undoubtedly the age of self-promotion. You used to have to wait for someone else to compliment you. Not anymore. Everyone, everything and everywhere is giving it the big one all day every day. Just tweet your praise for yourself until you've patted yourself so hard on the back that the skin's red raw and you've dislocated your shoulder. And then get busy retweeting praise of yourself that others have posted.

I was concerned that Brummies would get dragged into this orgy of self-love, but no, even in this climate, nothing. And God love us for keeping our dignity by keeping schtum about what's so great about us.

Are we missing out on opportunities because of all this? Quite possibly. Our civic leaders must despair at times, as they try to drum up inward investment by creating some noise about all that we offer. We're really not much help, are we? It's eccentric, I suppose, or perverse even; a bit like football supporters refusing to cheer for their own team. But that's just how it is.

Oh, how I love it. The city of a thousand trades, which found a thousand ways of not boasting about any of them. God, we're ace.

Alright, Muck? An Introduction

When Jon Bounds originally started our campaign he called it 'Birmingham: you might think it's shit, but I like it'. That was because most people seemed to think it was. Shit, that is.

"Birmingham? Urgh!" people said, "Birmingham is a grey wasteland on the way to the north."

To which Jon said, "Well, yes, but here's what's great about it."

Then, with much mulling, the people said, "Great? Really?" And Jon thought for a second and said, "Well… at least it's not shit".

It was not just these fictional people who felt like this. Some real people did too. Especially the real people who were paid to promote Birmingham: they thought it was shit and tried desperately to hide anything real about it.

"See," they said, "we have bistros at the foot of grade-one office space. If you squint, you could be in London."

There was a solution to the problem of Birmingham's image, they said. But it turned out to be the physically impossible act of banging a drum while blowing your own trumpet and shouting loudly about yourself. That and bulldozing the only truly interesting building in town to replace it with some more grade-one office space, with a bistro at the bottom.

Birmingham: it's Not Shit is eighteen years old. For all of that time we've tried to be different: we encouraged people to ride Birmingham's famous number 11 bus route for 11 hours on the 11th day of the 11th month. By riding buses without going anywhere, we thought we were getting somewhere. We dug up gold from the canals and found Tin Tin Duffy's bus pass. But then something strange happened: B:iNS became successful, if not popular, and if not well read, then at least celebrated. Proper grown ups, with titles like Parliamentary Under-Secretary for Creative Industries, name checked it in public speeches. Suddenly our founder was a local media hero with his celebrity measured and weighed, assayed and registered as the 14th most powerful person in the West Midlands. We got made mainstream, we got shit, so we killed it and relaunched.

Paradise Circus is our 'ongoing love letter to a battered city'. In a roundabout way, that means we are able to be critical of pretty much anything we choose (even the things that are good, sometimes), and through our previous book, our online stuff and even our stage show and number-one-hit record (UK Country and Western chart) we have taken the piss.

For this book, though, we're going to be nice. We're going to share with you the big and small things about the second city that make us smile. We hope you recognise some of it, that you learn something new, and that at least one essay gives you the same giddy feeling you get when you come out of the Queensway tunnels and can stop holding your breath. The idea is shamelessly stolen from JB Priestley who, in the years following the Second World War when there wasn't much to smile about, wrote a testament to the joy to be found in the simplest things in his 1949 book, *Delight*.

We can't offer every perspective, these are things that we find 'delight' us, that we remember, and that we can tell you about. All we promise is that we keep our eyes and minds open as we tell you why, and add a few jokes you'll only get if you're a Brummie.

There is no single correct narrative about the city we are connected to, apart from this one. Birmingham: it's not shit.

Jon, Jon, and Danny

Contents

Foreword by Adrian Chiles	5
Alright, Muck? An Introduction	8
Our Foggy Notions of History	13
Loving the 11 Bus	17
Scallops	21
Dexys Midnight Runners	24
Cobs	28
Your Local Balti House	31
Villa Park's Sarcastic Advertising Hoarding	36
Benjamin Zephaniah Turning Down an OBE	38
The Canals	41
The Ghost of Central Library	47
That Everywhere in Great Barr Looks the Same	51
The Electric Cinema	55
The Way Telly Savalas Looks at Birmingham	61
The Inevitable Perfect Disappointment of Star City	64
Seeing Fort Dunlop From the M6	67
Cliff Richard	70
Black Mekon	76
Digbeth	79
The Villa and The Blues	83
That Photo of Bill Clinton at The Malt House	91
The Flapper	95
Centre for Contemporary Cultural Studies	99
Taking Someone Up The Ackers	103
The Battle of Saltley Gate	106
Calling Roundabouts 'Islands'	111
Big Wednesday at Snobs	115
Mr Egg	122
Perry Barr Cars	125
Our Relationship to the Sea	127

Camp Hill Flyover	130
The Big Heart of Birmingham	133
The Reason We Don't Have an Underground	139
AB Fletcher	143
Lickey Road	144
Lenny Henry Doing David Bellamy on Tiswas	151
Spotting Birmingham on Telly and Film	156
Getting Bought Drinks in Perth, Australia	163
Tony Hancock Not Giving a Fuck About Birmingham	168
What Might Be Under Spaghetti Junction	172
Sutton Park	177
Our Tradition of Dissent	181
That Distinctively Nothing Skyline	186
The Jasper Carrott LP in Your Dad's Record Collection	191
The German Market, Yes, The German Market (Hear Me Out)	194
Boon (Series 1-3 only)	197
The Northfield Sunset, or The Corner of Lockward Road and the Sir Herbert Austin Way Bypass During the Months of June, July, and August at Around Seven O'Clock	201
The Lilac Time	204
A Small Enough City That You Can Learn It	208
The Austin Social Club	210
Mr Blue Sky	218

Our Foggy Notions of History

In the beginning was the word, and the word was 'this'll do, bab'.

A small band of people sat down and formed the homestead that would become Birmingham.

In a wooded glade beside a river that would become known as the Rea, near where what is now called Digbeth, they made camp. This river would provide the water of life. Eventually it would be a good place to pump shit out of factories into, to concrete over for years and then release fanciful architectural renderings promising to open it up again, but right now it was just for drinking, fishing, and bathing.

And pissing into. Pissing into and poisoning the drinking of those downstream in Aston, like those in Selly (not yet Selly Oak, having a tree wasn't noteworthy then) up the hill poisoned them. The new Brummies would have the last laugh in a millennia or so, but for now...

In the Domesday book, back in 1086, Birmingham is recorded as comprising nine households, worth 'about two goats', not to be confused with 'groats'. A 'groat' is a sort of medieval goat with larger horns and a bit of a cough. Hence the famous saying "Billy, t'goat's gruff"

So began the unfinished textbook *Paradise Circus's Half-Arsed History of Birmingham*, which remains unfinished, pretty much because there's little interesting recorded about Brum until the seventeenth century. Or more because what research I did contradicted the history I thought I knew and had written gags about. Including the stuff you've just read.

My reality tunnel of Brum's history didn't even survive basic online research. I had no idea that there was pre-history here but Wikipedia says there was. "Evidence from boreholes in Quinton, Nechells and Washwood Heath suggests that the climate and vegetation of Birmingham during this interglacial period were very similar to those of today". That's not a nice way to talk about historians, but they are doing good work here.

Birmingham's history is mostly unwritten, or at least ignored. The Industrial Revolution — the heavily edited version that focuses it directly here — is vaguely taught, and Carl Chinn does a fine line in people-centred near-history. Chinn's focus on populism however, means it dissolves into reminiscences of 'the pop man' and photocopies of old bus tickets whenever it meets the media: like the wave of drunken incapacity that hits you outside the warmth of a pub.

At least that's my excuse for knowing almost nothing about the history of the city. I don't think I am uncommon: people in Birmingham remain by and large ignorant of why the place is how it is. And if ignorance isn't bliss then it is at least liberating.

I grew up in the shadow of two types of history: the industrial might of weaponry in the IMI factory complex, and the genteel seat of oppression that was Aston Hall.

My grandad was convinced of two things about Aston Hall: that there is a secret tunnel to Aston parish church, and that the cannonball that broke the balusters on the stairs was fired from Cannon Hill.

Neither of those, as far as I can tell, is true. I base my guess on what a guide told Grandad when we were going around the Hall ("No, there isn't.") and on a vague knowledge of distance and physics. Even years after the Civil War, the best cannon could fire things less than a mile and Cannon Hill is around 15 miles away (or 19 if you check on Google maps — and there's currently heavy traffic on Bristol St). But Grandad never stopped believing, and never started researching, enjoying pub arguments about the cannonball for years after.

Text messaging wounded the pub quiz, the 4G internet killed it and a year of having to do them over Zoom desecrated the corpse, but before the recuperation of the question there was the long pub argument. Things that no-one would ever really know — without doing proper research, and no-one was going to do any of that — would be debated endlessly, ticking up when the personnel and the inebriation was just so. A rolling people-led inquiry into the nature of being, a collective hauntology of memories on the tips of our minds, a democratic but ineffable past that became a culture of the present. Single agreed truths put an end to all of that. History — firm history at least — is bunk.

I find sheer joy in Birmingham's less-than-clear grasp of

history: it's way more fun if you don't know what was going on.

Is this why Birmingham isn't shit? You don't want to know for sure.

JB

Loving the 11 Bus

The affection that the people of Brum have for just one of its 200 or so bus routes has been going round and round for way longer than you thought possible.

I have a commemorative reprint of a brochure advertising the delights of the Number 11 bus route — from 'the early 1930s' — that invites people to "see Birmingham's charming suburbs by 'bus", and presumably some of its least charming ones too as the joy of the thing is that it cuts right through us and opens us up to honest scrutiny.

Joining two routes — the 10 and the 11 — and becoming one in 1926, going all the way round pretty much straight away became something Brummies did: '25 miles for fifteen pence' as the guide says, and special Bank Holiday services. But why do we love it so much?

Is it the symbolic power of encircling a town? When Joshua brings down the walls of Jericho it's not the brass arrangement, it's the ongoing circumnavigation. Luckily we can go round and round as the city is not good at blowing its own trumpet.

The day trips and Bank Holidays were the sort of thing that local history stalwarts like Carl Chinn could base a tale on, homely and just at the edge of your lived experience (as well as your city). Carl could even combine this his other talent of telling us that the Peaky

Blinders did different things in real life, as no-doubt one of the 'real' ones did a circuit.

Almost all (over 80%) of public transport journeys in Brum are by bus. We, as a city, lack the cultural romance of the train or the solidarity of the Underground experience, this means that a bus route we all share can become part of our identity. If you're a young working class person in Birmingham — and statistically we have a greater density of these than other places in the UK — then it's likely to have formed some of your vespertinal journeys home from a job or out for a night.

My mate Gary, a man who loved Brum so much he had a crush on Claire Short, was an agency worker — all his jobs were crap and minimum wage, so he had only two questions when he was phoned up about a new one: "What are the hours?" and "Does the 11 go there?" With a daysaver he could get anywhere, almost without waking up properly in the morning.

It's said that Duran Duran wrote *Hungry like the Wolf* on the 11 bus; the band claim they wrote it in EMI's studios in London but given the amount of hunting you can do at peak time for a bus it's possible that it influenced the words. If it was written on the top deck it can't have been a full circuit as there's no way that writing the lyrics took two and a half hours.

There are undisputed cultural references, the bus features — although disappointingly isn't the main character in — Jonathan Coe's *Number 11* another of his satirical state of the nation novels, it inspired a Jethro Tull track and an internet novella (although that was us, does that count?).

I love the 11 bus, so much that I filmed an entire circuit to then speed it up to be five minutes long. I love it enough to have spent 11 hours going round and round. Of course I do, I'm a Brummie.

In 2008 I instigated a project called 11-11-11, the rules were: Get on the 11 at 11am (or as near as dammit) on 11 November (11/11). Get off the 11 at 10pm — 11 hours later — (or as near as dammit) still on 11/11.

And, because I wasn't doing it for charity, it confused people. I was not just being honest about how much I loved the bus route, but trying to explore why the people of the city all loved it too.

I wanted lots and lots of people that weren't thinking too hard about the *why* to enjoy it too. It helped me get a new perspective on the city, I wanted to spread that and was happy to talk to the media about it.

I hadn't remembered that 11 November was also Remembrance Day, so the hardest bit about talking to the BBC WM presenter was when, expecting to just do a bit of light nostalgic bus chat, I was quizzed about whether what we were doing was disrespecting 'our brave boys.'

The second hardest bit was not making a pornographic joke when asked 'What's your favourite: A or C?'

For a little while 11-11-11 produced some interesting things, which happily affected the bus itself not at all. Eventually some others did ride the 11 for charity and the spectacle was reset.

At various times the number 11 has been the longest bus route in Europe and we love that — a claim that can be allowed to 'big up Birmingham' as it's so mundane. It's a flipside to the 'more canals' one which is at once ridiculous and tongue in cheek, a thing we tell ourselves like a nervous tick.

Are Brummies genuinely proud of the Number 11? Do we love it because we can do so without our usual deprecating irony?

It might just be because it really is better to travel hopefully than arrive. If so Birmingham is the ideal place. Let's go round again.

JB

Scallops

What is a scallop? To a decorator, a scallop is a rounded pattern that you use to disrupt a clean line. To most people in the country a scallop is a small disk of seafood that Gordon Ramsay gets inordinately angry about before he smashes the plate with his fist and calls someone a 'cockdonkey'. But people from Birmingham know it's a delight, a treat on a treat, a dad's secret indulgence, and the best 50p you can spend on a cold afternoon.

An actual scallop is a small animal that lives in a shell, in fact you know what a scallop looks like. Ask any child to draw a sea shell and the scallop is what they'd draw. You know the one, the kind of shell that mermaids use as a bra. Sea scallops are difficult to transport, they don't stay fresh for long, also they soak up whatever impurity and contaminates that are nearby. So perhaps it's for these reasons the land-locked industrial Birmingham, ever resourceful and hating waste, began to use the spare word for something else.

The only other places to call the potato fritter, as some people wrongly call it, a scallop are some parts of Australia, which may blow my 'not being close to the sea' theory out of the canal. But I suspect the migration of English industry workers, the '£10 pom', imported the word, along with an aggressively large drinking ethic, and an undercurrent of petty racism.

Paradise Circus once conducted a scientific survey to use chip shop vernacular to map the disputed area of Greater Birmingham: we called it The Scallop Line. Our results showed that no one laughs when you refer to finding out what people have on their chips as 'crowdsaucing' but more importantly that our influence extends far into the Black Country. And if those from the Black Country could see beyond their mounds of faggots, scratchings and closed heavy industry, they would understand that too. We were sorry to piss on their chips (we know they'd rather have mushy peas) but they are in Greater Birmingham, because they love a scallop too.

Scallops, Birmingham scallops, are large slices of potato, covered in batter and deep fried. The ultimate go food: the correct way to eat a scallop is doused in salt and vinegar and with bits of chip paper stuck to it. It's important to note, nobody orders a scallop to eat as part of a meal, they are exclusively eaten on the way home from the chippy. Your first bite you get the grease and the crunch of the batter, part of your brain is very aware you've just consumed more calories than your average caveman managed to get in their entire lives. Your ancestors laugh at your bounty. Then when you hit the stage of thinking that, maybe, it's too greasy, and your stomach protests, the vinegar rushes in and the potato lets you know everything will be OK. If you're lucky the potato will be fluffy and scorching hot enough to make you make a hoooo hooo hooo sound trying to cool your mouth down by whispering a Santa Claus impression.

It's a dad snack, the secret scallop on the way home, one of those personal indulgences parents take occasionally to remind themselves the world can sometimes, just

sometimes, be about them. Recently I was at our local
chippy, I ordered some food, and as an afterthought.

"Oh, and a scallop for on the way home."

"Ha ha, you are Burt's son after all" the chippy maiden
nearly shouted. My dad is apparently a devout devourer
of the sly travel scallop. My dad's name is Dave by the
way, Burt is the local chippy's nickname for him for
reasons that are not mine to know.

There's something delightful in our stubborn refusal
to change the name of our fried treat, perhaps it's the
delightful way our accent makes the 'p' sound at the
end pop. Or it's just one of those shibboleths you aren't
aware of until it's pointed out: that off licences are not
called 'outdoors' anywhere else being another.

The secret scallop eaten hastily on the way home
on a grey Tuesday, the only trace being the grease
on your fingers and ming of vinegar will always be a
quintessential Birmingham experience.

DS

Dexys Midnight Runners

Postmodernism gets a bad press, literally. The British tabloids and also the British broadsheets, differentiated as they are by size of paper and coverage of soap opera rather than quality of reporting or ownership, both hate it. It gets bad press not just from those who blame its relativism for the creation of a post-truth society and lack of accountability in public life, there are also those who blame 'cultural Marxists' for their displeasure at small steps to equality. These people are all wrong, but there is a case to answer about how 90s bands such as Pulp were able to rehabilitate nylon as a fabric.

It isn't a lack of truth, postmodernism accepts that knowledge and value systems are socially-conditioned, accepting that they are products of political, historical, or cultural discourses and hierarchies. Postmodernism is, at its heart, about recognising control. And with Dexy's everyone — especially the other members — would recognise that this was all about the control of Bearwood's Kevin Rowland.

Before the 80s and 90s, people always meant what they said, we're told. No one lied, or if they did they resigned from the cabinet. Nor did anyone do irony. Credible bands, especially, meant it, maaan. But something about Dexys Midnight Runners in the late 1970s meant that you would look away and back quickly, hoping to catch them out. Surely they couldn't be so serious.

Birmingham was, at the time, a city dominated by modernism on the surface. But the cracks that let the light in, the rough edges to Madin and Manzoni's smooth lines, the stories of the people, were in the wreckage. Right up until the 90s, some scars remained: parts of town were still bomb-sites. Overgrown with weeds, fenced off usually, conscripted for use as car parks, these were the places that gave the depth to the narrative. They were tough places for a tough city; and now thanks to Dexy's it had a tough music.

Dexys Midnight Runners stood on that rubble — literally so in photoshoots — and worked harder than the workers on the track at Longbridge, worked to build something that wasn't all surface, was more than the sum of its parts. More strikingly, they didn't hide their intentions.

Usually, if a musical artist makes continual mention of their worth or brags of their attributes it is wise to take them with a healthy scepticism. I don't believe Dr. Dre was the original gangster, or that Ian Brown was the resurrection, any more than I think John Lennon was a walrus.

But Dexy's didn't just tell you they had soul, these were the young soul rebels that you were searching for. They built on the rubble of the soul that had gone before and were proud to show their workings, a Pompidou Centre of brass and history. It transported you back to 68, but it wasn't retro — it was *then* and it was massive. Dexy's were pop music in the sense of being popular, and serious bands didn't usually sustain that.

Rumour persists that the infamous *Top of the Pops* 'mistake' clip where Dexy's sing about soul legend Jackie

Wilson in front of a backdrop of darts legend Jocky, happened with the full knowledge of the band. Can you imagine Kevin Rowland — who dressed a band just so and worked them into the ground — would not have noticed and made a fuss? I believe Kevin did it: arch postmodernism.

Then a stylistic handbrake turn — Kevin sacked half the band, made Dexy's folkish and focused on the fiddle. To pull focus to their Irish heritage in a city still scarred by the pub bombings, to do something so brave and repeat the trick of releasing both ground-breaking and popular music is remarkable.

Look away for too long though, and Kevin has taken the dungarees to Oxfam and produced a three piece of perfect pop in preppy suits. Dexys Midnight Runners spent the decade turning their image on a sixpence, while being obsessed with notions of authenticity in themselves. The ultimate doublethink: band as conceptual art, but life-changingly wonderful and earnest at the same time.

They left different, but equally massive, legacies: *Come on Eileen* dominates a wedding dance floor, *Geno* expands to fill a nightclub of a sweaty type, *Don't Stand Me Down* is an adult pop masterpiece. Now older, even the post-reformation albums fill you with warmth. There isn't a spare note, there isn't a wrong step. This is the best band anywhere has to offer, and for a while it represented the place we come from. Before it vaulted the barriers at New Street and gave itself to the world.

Dexy's as they are now exist only on the tip of Birmingham: much like the Little Nibble café on

Bearwood High Street, which they namecheck in song. All of Bearwood, exists in a liminal state that is simultaneously too Birmingham to be Black Country and resolutely not in Birmingham. Which is why, when I came up with the idea for *Dexys Midnight Run* (always, always, come up with the name first and backfill what it actually is), I picked Dexy's MK I: meaning that this 5K run from the site of the Little Nibble to Birmingham city centre was to be performed not just at 12am, but in donkey jackets and woolly hats.

Not only is that the most impractical Dexy's outfit for a 5K, but it tallies with the story that Kevin Rowland would make the original band run and work out before practise. But more than that — it's the aggressive soul edition of the band that is really Birmingham. They dressed a little like Benny from *Crossroads*, after all.

The Run hasn't as yet happened. But original Midnight Runner and current Dexy's co-vocalist Pete Williams thinks it can: down the Hagley Road and finishing appropriately at Paradise Circus. Although he warns that proper donkey jackets are hard to come by, "it's all hi-viz neoprene these days". Authentic, to the last.

JB

Cobs

It was my first meal as a Brummie, on the day my parents dropped me off at university. Passed to me over the beer pumps and an antique brass drip tray, my first cob: a bread fist clutching at a mound of cheese, wrapped in cling film.

A simple cob from a big plate at the back of the bar is an absolute delight, but I don't want to fetishise the simple joy of these snacks. I'll leave that sort of work to the chalk boards of the street food stands, and I'll give those column inches to the food bloggers who obsess over the latest small plates concept in a pub you used to like (I'll give them an inch and they'll take a mile and then some). The cob is pure and simple, honest, and defies the sort of gentrification that needs me to hand raise an ode, low and slow, and serve it up on a slate.

The cob can be cheese (which always means cheddar). The cob can be ham (which means the very pink and very fatty slices from the deli at The Asda). Salad may be included at a push so long as it's a thick slice of tomato or a single leaf of a round head lettuce. Personally, I like a cheese and onion one, when I can get it.

The cob is drinkers' food. This is food on the hoof, necessary fuel between pints, which breaks the monotony of alternating salt n vinegar crisps and bags of scratchings. A cob is a commitment to a day at the bottom of a beer glass: we won't make it home for lunch, and dinner, if it comes, will be wrapped in paper after last orders. It's also a quiet enjoyment on a summer's day — to be munched on the bench outside, with a book or the paper. When you have no agenda to speak of, thinking about real food can be stressful and a cob becomes soul food, nourishing you in a cosy fog of stasis, allowing you to keep decisions at bay a little longer and ride the wave of a Saturday wasted and frittered away on nothing very much.

Cobs have been in decline for some time, so every time I find a pub with a plate of them it fills my heart. If I see a cob I always want one, and I'll usually buy one. When I do I feel like I'm putting a quid in the collection tin for the pandas or some other endangered species. If I don't speak up for the cobs, who will?

Cobs are definitely in trouble. The sort of pub that would do you a cob are the same sorts of pubs that are closing at a growing rate across the country, and that doesn't help. There have also been some murmurings that the cob is threatened by the dreaded 'health and safety' (sweating meat and dairy in plastic wrap on the counter all day is, to be fair, against pretty much every current food safety rule). Meanwhile the pubs that remain viable in the current market rely on food sales for a lot of their profit margin, and that food is more three-for-ten-pound-tapas than it is stick-a-quid-in-the-tin-and-grab-one.

The core problem, I think, that affects cobs is that they were usually a lovely little side-hustle. When I bought that first cob I noticed something a little weird. I asked for Guinness and a cob. The barman rang up a pint, took my fiver, split the change and gave some to me and dropped the rest in a pint pot under the optics. I went on to work in that pub and learned that this was one of several nice little earners we had for ourselves, outside of the control and oversight of the PLC that owned bricks, mortar, and stock control systems. The ham was indeed from The Asda and we bought it ourselves, made the cobs, and went out on the proceeds. In an increasingly managerial culture in pubs, and with an increasingly cash-free pub economy, it's hard to see how cobs can be offered without you taking a seat, placing your order at the bar and waiting for a slowly raised brioche bun with hand cut chips and a surfeit of fillings.

If you value 'real pubs', you probably value cobs, so when you see one grab it with both hands (the pub and the cob). Don't think about it — you don't need to, it's only a bloody cob — just sit on your bench with this book and take a bite, and then maybe have another pint or three and don't worry about anything too much, you can always grab some chips for tea on the way home.

JH

Your Local Balti House

When I said to my mom and dad that we should go for a balti, no one asked 'where?'. There's only one place we ever go to have a balti.

In the same way if you were to ask anyone where the best chippy in the country was, most people with a straight face tell you that it just so happens that it's the one within walking distance of their house. Yes, even yours, I know, I know it's won awards. My point is you don't eat at the best balti house, you eat at *your* balti house.

Akram's is busy on a Tuesday night. Even from across the road through the window partially obscured by the blue neon on the sign outside I can see twenty or so people, eating, drinking and fussing over each other in the way that families going out for a meal do.

I've had to come across the road for beer as, like most good curry houses, Akram's isn't licenced but welcomes you to bring your own. As I cross the road one of the brothers that run the palace, Niser, catches my eye. He's outside on a call, he smiles when he recognises me and waves. When we come in, Iftikhar, the eldest brother, is behind the counter, he glances up and smiles. When he sees us the smile turns up a wattage or two and he comes round to shake my dad's and then my hand firmly like old friends.

I have some memories of being very little and eating at curry houses. When we're sitting down my mom tells me that it was probably at a place that used to be in

Rubery. She doesn't pause to ask me or Dad, just orders six poppadoms from Ibrar, the third brother, as she's taking off her coat. A good rule of thumb for a novice is to count the heads and double it. The Himalaya (the curry house not the mountain range) used to be on land they rented from relatives, land that used to be a truckers' stop but now is a drive-through McDonald's.

Balti is a type of curry served in a small metal dish that may get its name from the Hindustani word for 'bucket' or from the Baltistan region of northern Pakistan. Baltis came to England in the 70s, their home being the main road between Sparkhill and Moseley now known as the 'Balti triangle'. If you're from Birmingham, especially south Birmingham, you've been going to your family's local balti house since you were very young.

The poppadoms come out and so does a gravy boat of mint yogurt and four small pots. I add the yoghurt to a plate along with the red stuff from one of the little pots and demolish my two in minutes, casually eating my dad's after that.

Iftikhar comes over and asks how everyone is. My dad asks after Mohammed, Iftikhar's dad, who semi-retired to India in 2007. My family have been coming to Akram's since 1994, when it was a small balti place above the Inshops Market in Northfield. From then Mom and Dad have been coming semi-regularly ever since, even spending four or five New Year's Eves in a row.

In 2000 the Akrams opened up a restaurant in Stirchley. Eventually they closed the Northfield restaurant, when I ask why Iftikar says, "Two things, Longbridge Rover plant closing, we lost a lot of trade then, and the thing that finally did us in was the bypass". I can see why, even though the car plants of Rover were winding down for years with wave after wave of redundancies and layoffs; when they finally closed in 2005 a lot of people who thought they were in a job for life found themselves unemployed. And the bypass effectively cuts off the Northfield estates on the west side of the Bristol Road from the high street. If not physically, after all it's just a road to cross, then psychologically. My mom says later "I just don't feel part of the village anymore".

Taking our starter order, Iftikhar calls me 'Craig' and offers me free shish kebabs. Craig is my brother, and he has good reason to remember him in particular over me. My brother was a troubled teenager with temper issues who once in a rage managed to tip over one of the heavy cast iron tables. The reason for the weight of the tables was to stop exactly that. My brother apologised later and ever since has been given a free shish kebabs starter. Other places would have barred him or even called the police. Mohammed Akram chose to be better, more understanding, and reach out using the universal language of food, a language my brother speaks fluently.

Our main course arrives, mine is what it always is, balti: meat no tomato, and a table naan that is literally the size of the table folded next to me like a delicious towel. For people unfamiliar with balti house techniques, most people use naan bread as a curry delivery system, edible cutlery. It is normal and encouraged never really to pick up any utensils. Personally the balti itself is merely a spicy and creamy garnish to the soft pillow of oily bread. When Iftikhar comes over to check I ask him how business is, he gets coy, and just gestures to the room.

"This is a Tuesday," he says.

"OK, but if I wanted to come on a Friday or Saturday? Would I have to book?" I ask, he just nods confidently.

"But many places are closing now, we're one of the oldest in the city, with the traditional black metal bowls, still open."

"You're still going, though. Say, what percentage of your customers are returning customers?"

"About 80-90%." he says after thinking.

"Why do you think they come back?"

"Why do *you* keep coming back?" he counters with a smile and continues "You're sitting in my living room. Everyone here we watched their kids grow up as they watched us grow up" My dad tells him he's retired now and he misses the people.

"I'd miss people, I'll work for another 40 years — I'd miss the banter."

I've often complained about people's reluctance to try new things especially as they get older, even if I understand it makes evolutionary sense. Why drink the water in the mystery lake over there when the water here, even though stagnant and with a weird copper taste, doesn't kill you dead instantly? But Birmingham peoples' loyalty to their balti houses is more than that.

As we leave my dad says thanks for everything. Iftikhar claps him on the back and says, "Of course, you're part of the family."

DS

Villa Park's Sarcastic Advertising Hoarding

I'm a Birmingham City fan, so I've always been happy to enjoy the bedsheet painting, cabbage throwing, Tim Sherwood employing comedy that comes straight outta Aston. But I actually have a lot of love for the outfit, I grew up in one of the rows of terraces in the shadow of the monolithic North Stand. I think of Villa much like the Harold Lloyd films I used to see on the telly, before the news until the BBC bought *Neighbours*. Lots of falling down, running aimlessly and even sometimes Paul Birch dangling from the clock on the Witton Lane Stand.

I used to go to a lot of Aston Villa games with mates and family, and there was always fun to be had — but looking back, two things outside of the matches really stand out as the comic events that make me love the Villa. By extension these delight me about Birmingham: because while we might have one of the most violent fan rivalries going, it's built on slapstick and fun.

Villa in the late 80s didn't win many trophies, which may have made their team photos a little dull — until in stepped sponsors Mita Copiers with a couple of their latest models and made sure that they looked like they'd won something: office equipment.

I wonder if Paul McGrath got free toner.

Villa's — long replaced — Witton Lane Stand had advertising hoardings across the front of the roof. Pretty permanent they were, because they were huge.

I recall MEB (the electricity board), Ansells "loads of everything" and, closest to the old massive Holte End terrace, was one for Taylor Steel (for those well-known consumer goods flat-rolled steel products — who goes to a match and decides they need some?), which promised "'Division One' Service"(note the scare quotes).

But then Villa — only five years after that European Cup win they like to mention — were relegated in 1987.

Rather than change the advert, they got someone to go up on a ladder and spray with the old stencil font "STILL" — making it "STILL 'Division One' Service" — which I always read with a sneer suggesting the rolled-steel products were better than the rubbish in front of you.

Which they surely were a few years later under Josef Venglos. More solid at the back anyway.

There wasn't a way of washing it off, so despite Villa's return to the top flight, this remained as long as the stand did: and it made me laugh every time I saw it. However no-one else has ever found it as funny.

JB

Benjamin Zephaniah Turning Down an OBE

You're not meant to answer your phone at work, you have to do it surreptitiously. Which is why, despite Benjamin Zephaniah phoning me up to tell me just why he'd turned down an OBE in the Queen's Christmas honours, I'm not sure why he did it. Phone me up, that is.

It was undoubtedly the right thing to do — good people do it, J.B. Priestley, Alan Bennett, Harold Pinter, David Bowie, Glenda Jackson as well as some absolute rotters like Evelyn Waugh the vile body who declined a CBE in the late 50s because he wanted a knighthood instead. It would have been fantastic to hear the reasons this great Brummie turned his from him directly. My attention was not only compromised by taking the call in an open-plan office but by the fact I was hiding something from Ben, or being politic about it at least.

Ben was under the impression that his turning down of the gong had led him to being voted Brummie of the Year — an award that he said "means more to me than any medal" — and I didn't want to disappoint him, because he'd come second. Second to a man whose achievements weren't as literary, a man who danced on the corner of the road in Small Heath with a walkman we were told had no batteries in.

I'm not proud that the inaugural Brummie of the Year was given to someone who was not being laughed with but at, and I shouldn't have allowed that nomination to reach the public vote, so perhaps we can say that Benjamin Zephaniah was the real 2003 Brummie of the Year and I can say "Sorry Malik". (In later years we abandoned the public vote altogether — after a year where we gave up the whole thing over what was described on Radio 4 by Mark Steel as being 'due to foul and abusive language' but was really about how something small could be overtaken — and now award the title on a whim, it's easier that way.)

But back to Ben, he was lovely, and had tracked my number down somehow and I knew who it was from the moment he spoke: the familiar warmth to his voice. Proud Brummies don't get a lot of coverage in the media today, in the early 90s they got almost none. Ben stood out and you knew some things: he was a Brummie, he was engaged and righteously angry about injustice, and he couldn't help mentioning the Villa. Most Brummies end up using part of their allocated message time to either ask us to 'shit on the VIlla' or support them, it's something of a tic.

"Me? I thought, OBE me? Up yours, I thought." Ben had written in The Guardian in a column he ended by telling Tony Blair to "stick it" — and you just know that if it had been ten years later he would have told David Cameron to stick to supporting West Ham too. But the most important thing he said, the one that makes me proud of the city that helped to shape him was this:

"I get angry when I hear the word 'empire'; it reminds me of slavery, it reminds me of thousands of years of brutality, it reminds me of how my foremothers were raped and my forefathers brutalised."

Stick it, elsewhere. Birmingham is not shit.

JB

The Canals

This is it: the one where we are contractually obliged to mention canals, and specifically the 'fact' that we have mor—

No, we're not going there. Not today.

The Birmingham Canal Navigations are extensive, interesting, and often buried by concrete, progress and mixed-use developments. As ever with Brummie things it's hard to define and measure the size of our canal network because the edges of the city are fuzzy and unknowable but, at around 100 miles, Birmingham has more cana—

That we have many canals is one of the things Birmingham has managed to enshrine in the popular consciousness. It is there in the noosphere alongside Spaghetti Junction, Julie Walters, Black Sabbath, and Dairy Milk chocolate as one of the Birmingham things. And when any outsider calls on this, as Brummies we reflexively answer with pride "that's right, more canals th—"

The canals, and the way we talk about them, delight and amuse me because, branch by branch, lock by lock, our waterways exist on a spectrum between outright neglect and bougie excess.

We sell the canals as something of a tourist attraction, which is a rather odd thing to do. In and around the Convention Quarter (the square kilometre or so from the Arena, past the ICC, to Mailbox via Gas Street

Basin and then back via Broad Street and Brindley Place) there is a certain amount of respectable and anodyne waterside entertainment to be had. Here, the too-tight-jeans and shiny-shoe-wearing visitors can follow in presidential footsteps with a pint of real ale at The Malt House, while the ladies laugh and eat a waterside salad. For those keen to explore the canals themselves, the 'water bus' will shuttle you from the Pitcher and Piano to Pizza Express, or for less than a fiver the more adventurous tourists can stay on to do a full lap of the various new build apartment blocks. Their reward at the end: a pint of Peroni at All Bar One.

Step a yard outside of this space and things quickly become edgier for the well-heeled and pearl-clutching classes. In the corner of Old Turn Junction, King Edwards Road shoots over the water in front of the Arena, its bridge making a shelter where pockets of men gather to drink large bottles of cider. In truth they're no more threatening than the braying chaps and chapesses a boat length away, but this isn't the continental style drinking that a regional development officer has in mind when they make a big play about the city's café culture. A little further on, the greebos, the crusties and the goths cling on to their own waterside oasis at the Flapper: the indie darling pub, a local institution for sub-cultures and live music, all of it very much at risk of being turned into flats.

Follow the canal in any direction from Brindley Place and you'll see a similar story: the very safe, cookie cutter, waterside bars quickly pass, and the canals begin to peel away layers of history and show stories about Birmingham as it was, and as it is.

You might find a pub or two, and if you do you'll probably find a story too — like the story of the Fiddle & Bone. On the opposite side of the Arena to the Flapper, the Fiddle & Bone was once a much loved jazz and folk pub, the sort of thing that attracts people to an area. Unfortunately the people who were attracted to the area decided that actually living somewhere cool and interesting was a bit of a pain, so they forced the place to shut in 2003 for being too noisy. The pub sat empty for a long time but is now reopened as The Distillery, a place where you can have a laugh over a salad and a San Miguel while looking, quietly, at the canal.

Pushing on deeper, away from the regeneration, you begin to be rewarded with a real sense of the canal network's historic purpose as old factories, some derelict, some still in use, crowd you in. There is scant to orient you to all the history which I've always thought was a shame, but when you find something it's always a gift.

A little further up from The Flapper, a plaque on the wall identifies Saturday Bridge.

The bridge is almost unnoticeable at street level — it's a flat continuation from Sandpits to The Parade. From the top of a bus or the pavement you might get a glimpse of the Arena and realise that for a second you were borne over water. From beneath, on the towpath, Saturday Bridge is a short tunnel under the road.

Always read the plaque: Saturday Bridge, it says, got its name from the practice of paying boat workers at this point on the canal on Saturdays. Up at street level, they used to queue here for the Job Centre Plus. It's a quirky piece of irony, a geographical comment on the post-industrial economy of Britain and Birmingham.

We often think of modernisation and regeneration along the canals as taking the form of flats and loft apartments, but it takes on more practical forms too.

An industrial chimney is built first and foremost for a function: to carry off an exhaust gas, and to allow the intake of fresh air. Later, once you have a chimney that will do this right, you might turn your attention to adornment, to designing a chimney as an aesthetic task, and to making a statement. But then, much later, if the chimney loses its function it becomes two things: a vestige and a symbol of an industrial past. In the modern day the stacks of the Industrial Revolution are reduced purely to their secondary, aesthetic, function acting as iconography for industrial heritage. These are the dormant, sleeping, dreaming spires to the empty cathedrals of industry and they have no value beyond sentimentality.

And yet…

Look properly at the old chimney stacks of the works that bank onto the canal and you might notice some stacks are crowned with phone masts. It seems obvious really: the stack affords rare height in a flat area, so of course the phone companies would want to use the redundant chimneys to house their antennae. The dreaming spires are stirring. Stop, look and imagine signals pouring through those masts: photos, emails, calls all pumped high into the sky, drawing fresh bits and bytes behind them, knitting together a blanket not of smoke but of data, a digital smog from that loom of towering brick built chimneys. The city's tech industry boosters have for some time tried to pitch the idea of a Birmingham innovation hub known as 'Silicon Canal', and here it is, an artery for data rather than startups that traces the same lines that brought coal to furnaces.

There are more obvious things to spot for a wanderer on the canals. Abandoned factories provide acres of canvas for graffiti, while many boats will carry 'Roses and Castles' style folk art and often elaborate gardens too. Further from town, factories give way to hedgerows and wildlife is the walkers' reward.

The pedestrian infrastructure of the canal clearly breaks down the further you get from the city, solid gravel paths becoming boggy tracks, yet they remain a viable way to walk or cycle through much of Birmingham. It's arguable whether or not this is pleasant, though.

Much of the canal network is bothered by fly-tippers (you could open a branch of SCS with the sofas you might find on a stroll along the Grand Union, and certainly the sale would never end) and things can often feel a little sketchy down the cut. You're never more than a metre from a discarded whippet canister, and for long stretches of a canal walk your only companions will be an occasional grouping of gaunt and grey men, passing a saggy joint or swigging cheap beer from black bags.

I should say, however, that I've never experienced an ounce of trouble when walking, running, or cycling along our waterways. I should also, though, reflect that I am a bloke and that this affords me a whole bunch of privilege. The worst thing that has happened to me on a canal was when I ran around the corner by the Gun Barrel Proof House in Digbeth, disappointing a flasher who, hoping for a lady, wasted a shot of his barrel on me.

The canals are a weird source of civic pride for something that most of us hardly think about at all, which few of us use and which are full of threat and low-key menace, or over-priced lager and ciabatta sandwiches.

They point to our history, and reflect on our present and our future. And there are, perhaps, more of them here than there are in Ven—

JH

The Ghost of Central Library

Of all the lies we get told as kids perhaps the kindest is 'there's no such thing as ghosts', but even as kids we don't believe it. The adults that tell us that are unafraid and only a tiny bit sad so we allow ourselves to be soothed.

Of course as adults we know better, a lifetime of habit, mistakes, triumphs and disappointments later and everywhere we go has a lattice of memories overlayed, a spiderweb of experience ready to catch the unwary. Certain perfumes will put us teenager-hard back into soft arms, the electric hum of your parents' old telly heard years later and hundreds of miles away can still wash you in comfort, and long gone friends can live again in a stranger's shrug or the curve of their smile.

Sleep is hardly an escape from the ghosts. Personally I only ever dream of the dead, sometimes all they seem to want is to check in, but more often they beg me to move on, tell me it's OK, and there was nothing I could have done. I probably dream of more than ghosts but it's these lessons that I will never learn that are the only ones I seem to remember.

The Central Library was a dirty weird monument of jagged lines surrounded by a labyrinth of concrete, noise and graffiti. The best description would be 'an upside-down ziggurat' if that also did not involve explaining what a ziggurat is. It was a home to me, however you chose to describe that word. I would spend hours discovering writers I still love, developing what little musical taste I have in the CD section, and browsing the internet when all that was on it were four Star Trek forums and a single picture of a woman with no top on. The library was where I planted myself, while my roots explored the world outside and turned my face to the sun.

When they finally pulled it down it happened over months. Day-by-day and in public the carcass would have new chunks bitten out of it. Until one day they knocked a hole through the middle, leaving it splayed open like the inquisition stripping their victim, not only of their life, but any chance of dignity. I'm told the hose that sprays water during a demolition is to stop the brick dust from igniting. But, to me, it was hard not seeing it as the city crying.

Ghosts in folklore are said to be the creation of violent or traumatic acts, things so terrible they can never be forgotten. Pulling down Central Library and displaying its innards was a wound we all felt. An act of cultural cruelty and aesthetic ignorance.

But you can't kill love with a bulldozer.

The Central Library has gone, but only physically. It's alive everywhere it matters not least in the hearts of the people that loved her. Photos still exist and are regularly shared and adored, artists still respond to its shape and story with prints, tote bags, badges, paintings, and in love letters like this. There's at least one documentary about it and even more entries in reference and history books. In fact if you didn't know it had been knocked down you could still be trying to see the building that appears on our tea towels.

The area is redeveloped (from the Latin *redevelop: capitalism's habit of making things more shit.* not to be confused with mass production: *capitalism's habit of making more shit things*) but every day someone will post on social media a picture from the same quarter square mile with some inane caption like 'DAAMN BIRMINGHAM YOU IS LOOKING FINE TODAY' and the same idiots that took nearly exactly the same photo yesterday will give it a like, and the cycle continues. A circle-wank of insecurity. 'One Chamberlain Square' doesn't look good, it just looks clean. My pet theory is that people are not responding to the anodyne architecture that replaced it, they're responding to the love for the old library, they're responding to the love for the old place that has seeped into the ground like mercury. A love so deep not even a corporate architect could erase it.

The ghost of Central Library is everywhere. We carry the ghosts of our own making with us, sometimes they can cut like fresh paper, or crush like dead rocks, but they can also heal, comfort, and if we try, push us to be the people we hoped we could be back when we were told ghosts didn't even exist.

I carry the ghost Central Library with me, I see its shape in the negative space of Birmingham's skyline, I feel its yellow lights humming against my eyes whenever I nap somewhere I shouldn't, and it's what I smell whenever I'm near dust or old vanilla. It's not healthy to hold on to the past too much, but it's perhaps just as bad to forget where you came from.

I know, years from now and perhaps a thousand miles away from Birmingham, that when I die and they crack my chest to read my entrails my heart will be red, but also grey, and shaped like an upside-down ziggurat.

DS

That Everywhere in Great Barr Looks the Same

Birmingham is the highest point west of the Urals. Great Barr is as hilly as all hell, the pubs are all big and on the verge of kicking off, or big, closed, and on the verge of burning down. I don't think there's a trendy coffee shop for miles, and good luck with seeing any art other than a tribute act since The Kings isn't there any more for basket meals and appearances by The Barron Knights.

During the Second World War, in many places they removed road signs to confuse any Nazi paratroopers that might land. In suburban Birmingham they just built road after road of identical semi-detached houses that wind round on each other in a way that makes you sure the estates were planned not by the Public Works Committee of the Council but by M.C. Escher.

Never sure where you are until you turn a corner onto a wider road and see a landmark, lost on a walk of shame, navigating by incline alone: the sheer delight in being able to get lost yards from your front door is a feeling akin to driving fast over the hump-backed bridge by Highcroft as you race into Erdington.

Did the city planners just see one semi-, with a box room at the front that stretched the definition of 'bedroom' even in those days when people were smaller, and say: "Yeah, thousands and thousands of these randomly all

around the place, around the outskirts of town please."?
Sort of. And it's to our credit that they did.

A 1919 survey estimated that 14,500 new homes were needed in the city within three years — a huge amount by today's standards, but we had around 40,000 back-to-backs and 200,000 people living in slums.

But then, between the wars, Birmingham built more than 51,000 new council houses — more than any local authority in the country outside London (as we always have to say when talking about anything to do with scale).

Nearly all those homes were built, not where people were living in those slum back-to-backs, (although with a lovely sweetshop on the corner) but on farmland around the outside of town. The city grew new 'cottage suburbs' like the rings of a tree.

The Perry Barr Estate was brought into the City of Birmingham in 1928 and then filled with 5,000 council houses which were built in three years. In ten there were almost 10,000: with Kingstanding, Erdington, Witton Lodge Farm and Oscott College joining it and confusing our fictional German paratrooper even more.

In South Birmingham, you could now get lost in Northfield or Weoley Castle too.

At this stage it did very little to help those in poor housing, high rents meant a skilled and better-off working class — many who moved into the city — were the ones who now lived on the new estates.

Lots of these houses were 3B type "with parlour, living room, scullery and three bedrooms": most now often becoming houses with through-lounges, extended kitchens, drives at the front and — in my dad's case — a nightmare post-apocalyptic tableau of artificial grass populated by gnomes with various bits broken off out the back.

Decorate or desecrate them how you like, you can't make those houses, trees and grass verges look like anything but themselves; and crucially each other. With few landmarks and no obvious plan as to how the roads related to each other (those hills again), those of us who spent a good deal of time in our suburbs had to evolve other strategies to find our way around.

From a very early age, we learnt to navigate the outer reaches of Birmingham by pubs and nothing else: for in the suburbs they were the only true way to tell where you were. Going up the Queslett Road, the signs were all you had; each by itself — double fronted and on an island — looked pretty much identical. The Old Horns, The Trees, The Deer's Leap, The Queslett, if you parachuted in there would be little chance of you knowing which way to go to The Scott Arms. Navigation by pub was further complicated by the 90s fashion of changing their names, and the 00s habit of turning them into large Chinese buffets. Like a pub timelord, you were conditioned to knowing the names they used to have before you were born, let alone before you had ever been inside.

Everywhere looking the same taught you pubs, it taught you history. Getting lost is part of Brum's special charm, and a reason why it's not shit. Not at all.

JB

The Electric Cinema

The Electric Cinema is very flammable.

There was a time when all cinemas were highly flammable. In olden times all buildings were tinder boxes, of course, but cinemas had the added flair of being full of nitrocellulose (that's film stock to you and me), a substance capable of spontaneous combustion and which, once lit, actually feeds itself by handily producing oxygen while it burns.

The Electric Cinema opened in 1909 and still has not caught fire.

I first knew The Electric Cinema in its late 1990s incarnation. Painted in dappled burnt orange, with zany 80s signage, and featuring the terrifying art installation Thatcher's Children by John Buckley (a series of macabre mannequins, hanging out of windows on the same level as the old New Street Station exits) it was quite an intimidating proposition from the outside — like the weird new kid at school with the too-big leather jacket, dyed hair and anachronistic musical tastes inherited from his older brother who lives away (is he in prison? The Army? Dead?). But much like that weird new kid, if you could get close to it, it was actually lovely. Weird but lovely. At The Electric in the 90s they had homemade cake alongside their terrifying statues.

It's the oldest working cinema in the country. This is a fact. It's a fact that is frequently disputed, but it's a fact nonetheless: The Electric is older than the rest, and also has not burned down yet.

In the early 2000s The Electric closed down. It left a hole in Birmingham's cinema scene as there were few other venues programming anything much outside of mainstream multiplex fare. It also left an empty and somewhat combustible building on a plot of land bang in the city centre.

Empty buildings have had a habit of burning down in Birmingham, especially those that might be in the way of progress (progress in the form of city centre apartments and mixed-use developments). It's a fate that has befallen many old pubs, factories, and cinemas too so you'd have been forgiven for expecting to read some sad news about The Electric back in 2003 but, like a phoenix without flames, The Electric came back from closure unharmed, renewed even. Restored and resplendent in an art deco makeover-cum-restoration, The Electric surged back into business in 2004 with a mix of mainstream movies, arty stuff, and they even still had cake!

Under the ownership of a chap called Tom Lawes, The Electric saw its way through to its centenary year in 2009. My co-author Jon Bounds attended a special 100th birthday party at the cinema and reported back to us on the BiNS website:

> *Tom showed a great deal of the refurb work that's gone into turning the cinema back into an inviting place in recent years — the roof and the plumbing seem to have contributed to it pretty much falling down. I felt a bit uncomfortable with the way in which the previous own-*

> *ers/management were obviously seen. Business-wise they were crap no-doubt, but for a while at least they brought all manner of esoteric, odd, niche and arty films to Brum — I have fond memories of dozing during triple bills of Italian films in the mid to late 90s.*

To further celebrate, Lawes put together a film about the history of British cinemas, and The Electric's place in that story. *The Last Projectionist*, which came out in 2011, has been described variously as an award-winning documentary and a "nostalgic advertorial" for The Electric but further cemented Lawes's stock as Birmingham's charming man of cinema.

The Electric of this era brought a sense of occasion back to going to the cinema. As a visitor you wouldn't need to know the deep lore of the place for it to feel special — the history is there in the bricks, it's palpable. Beyond the *mise en scene*, The Electric worked harder than most for you to have a nice time, with little extras like bar service to your seat and the big squishy sofas at the back of the room. Chains such as Everyman — which opened a Birmingham cinema in 2015 — compete with this luxury experience, though, offering more and squishier sofas, drinks and food service, and that weird thing where a handsome man stands at the front of the room before the film to introduce it. Everyman's interior designers have reached for opulence: it's all dark wood panelling and chintzy lights, a sort of speakeasy 1930s vibe — like someone poured the aesthetic of a George Clooney Nespresso ad into a multiplex — but they'll never have the history The Electric has and so Birmingham's Everyman will forever be a concrete unit in the Mailbox doing dress-up.

57

Slightly more expensive seats and a slightly more curated programme made this era of The Electric a pretty safe bet for date nights for the well-heeled, and the restoration style of the refurb perhaps helped it catch an updraft of cool cachet, as the whole vibe chimed well with the growth of interest in all things vintage.

Whilst it relied on bankable fare from blockbusters that were lighting up the box office, it kept a toehold for itself and for the city in the more artistic and alternative end of cinema too. For example, my all-time favourite cinema trip was to see *Oxide Ghosts* by Michael Cumming at The Electric.

Oxide Ghosts is a documentary about the Chris Morris TV show *Brasseye*, which was made with Morris's blessing, on condition that it was only ever shown in cinemas and only if Cumming physically took it there himself and spoke about the film at length before and after it was screened. The whole setup for this is an incredible piece of self-curatorship by Chris Morris which, for me, beats even Morrissey's insistence on having his autobiography published under Penguin Classics as an example of artistic shit-housing. *Oxide Ghosts* could only really show somewhere like The Electric because The Electric can make decisions locally, flex its programming to suit, and is big enough to make the showing worthwhile but also small enough to sell out such a weird event.

This is what is so delightful about this historic place: it allows Birmingham to stay connected to a world of film outside of what's on offer at Great Park Rubery or Star City. And as a fixture of Birmingham for over 100 years, almost everyone has stories about going there, but if your dad has stories from the 70s they're mucky ones…

If the post-2004 Electric was loved, its new owner, Lawes, was too. Saving The Electric (and serving fancy gin and lovely cupcakes) keeps you onside with the Evening Mail and would also go on to delight the slightly breathless #WowBrum faction of content posters who emerged in the 2010s to catalogue the nightlife and culture of our city. But Birmingham does love to build people up and knock them down, and some people like to bring their own hammer to help. When the Covid-19 pandemic forced cinemas to close, Lawes made his staff redundant when they could have been kept on under furlough and was roundly called out for his behaviour. Worse would be still to come, as the website for the cinema was replaced with a message that read:

> ***The future of The Electric Cinema Birmingham faces an even bigger issue than that of Covid due to the impending end of its 88 year lease.***
>
> ***As the freeholder has yet to make a decision about its plans for Station Street, we are not currently in a position to reopen the cinema.***
>
> ***This uncertainty has also meant we have been unable to apply for the Cultural Recovery Fund or other financial support to assist us financially through the period of closure.***

The subtext in the note: they're coming for this historic and flammable building, I've lost.

At the time of writing, it seems that The Electric will continue again. A new hero has emerged, in the form of Kevin Markwick, who already owns a not-quite-as-old cinema in East Sussex, and has promised to reopen the cinema and restore it to its former glory days, presumably by reinstalling Thatcher's Children.

As we saw earlier, in Jon's account of The Electric's centenary, Tom Lawes had been more than happy to criticise the business acumen of The Electric's prior stewards, but it seems he may have succumbed to the same problems in the end. It will always be true, though, that he saved the UK's oldest working cinema from dereliction (and probably a fire). As with a disgraced pop star or movie maker, even if ultimately we feel let down by Tom Lawes we have to say: his work still speaks for itself, his work still stands — and The Electric still stands, un-burnt down, flickering its story onto the screen again and again, its projector a light that never goes out.

JH

The Way Telly Savalas Looks at Birmingham

It was remembered the other day, I saw the practised incredulity float past on Twitter. And of all the things that are permanently forgotten in order to be revived, 'the Kojak film' is one that gives good remember every time. Birmingham: It's Not Shit was responsible for perhaps the first great remembering, which, for me at least, was a discovery and, in my defence, I haven't forgotten it since.

Like all good dramas, all of the action was contained within a TV studio. Or two studios. In one, Telly Savalas jetting into London, settling down in a booth and knocking off a number of local 'Looks at' film voice-overs in a day, then jetting back off (the film forgotten, Birmingham never known). The second, where the first great remembering is taking place, within the BBC Birmingham bit of the Mailbox.

I was working for the BBC, a chap called Russell Parker was working in the editing suites a couple of floors below. He had not only seen *Telly Savalas Looks at Birmingham* but had managed to run off a DVD copy, and dropped me an email. I went down into the bowels of The Mailbox and picked it up.

The plot: Telly Savalas, American actor most famous for *Kojak* and *The Dirty Dozen*, has come to Birmingham (he hasn't) and is sending you a sort of video postcard that will extol the virtues of the city. Like a good DJ he's talking to just one person, telling you how he arrived (he didn't) at 'apple blossom time' (it wasn't), took 'an elevator to the top of one of the city's tallest buildings' (he didn't) and 'dallied in Dale End' (he didn't, no one did, no one ever has — including the cameraman who took less than a couple of seconds of a shot there).

So he's lying to you, he never did come across an over-40s disco-dancing competition in Cannon Hill Park, but at least he's doing a stand up job of pretending to, right up until he breaks into character and signs off with "Yes it's my kind of town. So long Birmingham, here's looking at you!" as the camera zooms out, implying he's being pulled into space from his car on the Aston Expressway.

But it was, and remains, marvellous. I was astounded, especially by the way they'd padded out an already short film with the disco-dancing. I cut a very short edit which I then compressed to all hell (the most the web could take at the time) and stuck it up online. It went big, articles in the paper, the BBC local news calling me up, only for me to be able to wave at them across the office. Kojak looking at Birmingham had been remembered, and we mainly wanted to meet the disco-dancers, especially the woman. We didn't find them at the time.

I did get a call from the guy that owned the film and expected to get hit with some sort of takedown. But no, he took me for lunch and even paid for the music rights needed to put my edit online legally. (This also happened in the Mailbox, which didn't strike me as too strange at the time, until a friend wrote a novel set entirely within the walls of the place. Then I had to get out.)

Richard Jeffs had acquired the Baim Films archive which included TSLAB and TSLAP (Portsmouth: "I don't know of another place where so many famous people have had streets named after them"), as well as TSLAA (Aberdeen: "trouble with tartan is unheard of"). He told me that they were what was known as 'quota quickies': essentially cinemas were mandated to show a number of British films, and shorts like this were the absolute cheapest they could make. They would be shown as support to a film and then quickly forgotten. Forgotten as they were of little value: only much later would we discover the value in remembering them.

Years later, I would bump into Russell Parker again in the back room of The Victoria and he would introduce me to someone whose nan had been in an over-40s disco-dancing competition in Cannon Hill Park: yes, it was our dancer. Parker truly is the midwife of remembering Kojak looking at Birmingham.

What is it about the film that makes remembering it so perfect? Is it the music, rumbling urgent De Wolfe library selections? Does it capture a special moment that makes it perfectly nostalgic? Is it the narration, excitedly quotidian and certain to inspire the vocals of an experimental jazz LP, if it hasn't already? Is it the incongruity of Telly Savalas, cynical cool American, visiting (he didn't) the technicolour greyness of 1970s Birmingham?

I think it's a combination of all of these: it's not that Telly Savalas looks at Birmingham that delights, it's how he does it. Remembering things? Here's looking at you.

JB

The Inevitable Perfect Disappointment of Star City

In the 1979 film *The Warriors*, a delegation from the eponymous gang fight their way through the boroughs of New York to get home. When they finally get back to their home turf you see them visibly relax, they know the ground, weapons come easily to hand, and the sun begins to rise. But a rival gang follows them and confronts them on the beach. Ajax tells the leader of the rival gang, "We figure we see the ocean, we're home, we're safe."

I don't like saying that I don't know how to drive, not that I'm embarrassed — people that know me well tell me that it'd be a mistake for me to drive, something about impulse control and being easily bored. No, I don't like saying I don't know how to drive simply because we don't know if that's true. I've never tried to drive: I might be brilliant. Nevertheless there are many advantages to being a permanent passenger, there's lots of lovely buttons and switches to press, I never sleep so well as when my head is smushed against a moving window, and road beers give you a significant head start on the fun.

The main advantage though is not having to pay attention to the motorways, which are uniformly boring. At any party containing two or more dads their conversation will inevitably turn to the minutiae of the motorway system, which exits they took, their favorite shortcuts, and the varying strengths and weaknesses of essentially identical stretches of road.

To me it all looks the same, which is why the occasional landmark is important and in the case of seeing the playful primary colours and friendly curved roof of Star City almost totemic. I figure I see Star City, I'm home, I'm safe.

But while the sight of Star City is easily accessible by anyone coming to Birmingham from the M6, actually getting to Star City from most places in Birmingham itself is a lot more difficult. Getting into the city centre and home again on public transport is a pain in itself, but accessing the other side of town? Nigh impossible without spending the sort of taxi money no one has. If you come by narrow boat though, Star City has its own mooring. The planners seriously overestimated the areas of the venn diagram in which 'canal boat owners' and 'regular casino attendees' overlap. At this distance I built the idea of Star City into some sort of adult Disneyland, a mini Vegas, an ADHD Shangri-La of lights and noise. Apart from a couple of nights working the door in one of the clubs just after it opened I've never been.

Star City was opening in the year 2000 as part of a regeneration scheme for the area, the cinema was the biggest in Birmingham at the time and they flew in the world's most fuckable Batman George Clooney and celebrity racist Mark Wahlburg to promote the film *The Perfect Storm*. A film that tells the story of two unfeasibly handsome fishermen that get caught in conditions that could only exist if a series of unlikely circumstances come together in just the right way.

The regeneration of the area around Star City never really happened, today it sits isolated in the middle of several industrial parks. Nechells remains one of the most underfunded and deprived areas of Birmingham, and with youth services cut to the bone it's no wonder local young people flock to the area which puts off even the most adventurous punter from going there at night. Pictures in the local paper of a twelve year old carrying a machete don't help either.

A Perfect Storm, of shit.

Star City fulfils none of the promises made by its glitzy image, it's tatty around the edges, the centrepiece escalators have never both been working at the same time, and a lot of the units are empty, with more in a state of just opening or just closing.

But reality doesn't matter too much, sometimes the dream is just as important and to me I see the lights and glamour from the M6 and I figure I'm home, I'm safe.

Disappointment doesn't matter, I still dream of a mini Vegas just a couple of bus trips away. Perfect storm of shit as it is now, it has potential. And one thing Birmingham does well is potential. So I'll stay here in the passenger seat, face smushed against the window with neon dreams and a promise of a better future.

DS

Seeing Fort Dunlop From the M6

My wife says that as soon as you get on the M42 from the M40 going north the standard, the type, of driving changes and people are more aggressive. I agree, it's true; but it feels good to me, it feels like home.

You can't live in Birmingham without having a relationship with the car. And if you drive around much you get a relationship with the roads too, one that should feel comfortable. Not too long ago, coming from an unfamiliar direction, a diversion, tired and attempting to avoid the traffic building up between the Scott Arms junction and Spaghetti, I ended up going the wrong way. And then, turning round at Junction 7 — the motorway island I'd driven round more than any other — about to give up and face that traffic, I did it again.

Back onto the M6 going towards Ikea, I decided I could swing round and hit the M5 and, in the end, got where I was going without adding much more than half an hour to the journey. But I knew it was significant: going the wrong way on Spaghetti Junction was a sign that the pathways in my brain that mean I don't have to think about some things, they just happen, had been re-wired.

Some years back I was working in Worcester, driving every day from Moseley, and would often 'wake' as I parked at the office with little knowledge of how I'd got there. If interrogated, it seemed dangerous, that you could drive at 70 for miles, that you could drive down the motorway, and have no real clue about it, but

I was aware, I was safe. What I was doing was being on autopilot because I'd trained myself. And now, the pathways that held the old ways, what were the usual ways, were gone.

I'd already stopped knowing which pubs were the decent ones in town. I'd long since had to use maps to find out where the 16 stopped to get back to Hamstead. The new New Street is not just a maze to me because it's a maze to everyone: it's because it's not *my* station.

There were times when, in my New Street, just coming down the escalator and seeing the departure boards would feel like taking off a restrictive jacket. Deciding whether to get a can for the train, meeting people there in the mass watching the letters flick over, or standing — bag between ankles — before going down to the platform, would be a Proustian rush far better than the texture of a bag of Porky Puffs or the smell of a long-marinated beer mat.

The place has always changed, too fast for some, but I'm not just being nostalgic. I think I'm reflecting that it's not the place that changes so much as us. And if it's an effort to move around, you have to acknowledge that: because you're acknowledging that your reflections are a distortion in the fairground mirror of your memories.

The world is changing more quickly now than it seems it ever did. Even in the 80s I remember bomb sites, long-gone factories behind rough fences, compacted dust on which to park cars or cut through. The desire-paths of our urban life, the secret passages and hollow ways through unwanted and overgrown spaces. Take the gully, leave by the side gate at Perry Barr station to avoid the ticket collector, there's a hole in the fence along here. The short cuts are the hardest to learn.

But there are different emotions now, those of the return. Seeing Fort Dunlop coming up on the right, testing the view against your memories. Later you pass Villa Park, flick the Vs if it's safe to take your hand off the wheel, and then you can see the gas towers of Saltley, you count up the landmarks and slip back into it.

There's nothing like coming home.

JB

Cliff Richard

Cliff Richard is not from Birmingham; reason for celebration enough some might think, but they are cynics and have no place in this discussion. A fleeting mention of Cliff Richards — I always pluralise, a tic with an origin I'm not sure of — makes me think of Birmingham and smile, for Cliff is somehow part of Birmingham.

The parallels are huge. We, as a city, are Christmas — we shine and glitter in a gaudy way. Cliff is too — he's had four Xmas number ones to our one. We both love Eurovision — Cliff's two appearances to our one outranks us. We both love women's tennis, and neither of us get much sex.

When things aren't going well for either of us, Cliff and Birmingham are drawn together against the elements. Celebrity indoor tennis tournaments give you something to do when the hits aren't exactly flowing like water, and Birmingham can hold them like no other, when the newly-built arena isn't being used for anything good.

For me the symbiotic relationship between the city and the singer dates back to 1972. Cliff released a heavily religious single into a chart that was topped by Don 'the other one' McLean's *American Pie* and Nilsson's *Without You*.

"Jesus, won't you come back to earth?" the song implored, which was the same thing that people said to the council when they again announced that Brum was bidding for the Olympics. It's a very Brummie exclamation when you think about it: 'Jesus, are they digging up Corporation Street again?', 'Jesus, what's Mike Whitby paid Capita to do now?' or simply 'Jesus, have you seen that film where Cliff Bloody Richards drives a hovercraft under Spaghetti Junction?'

The 45 peaked at just 35 in the UK Singles Chart, Cliff's second lowest placing in 15 years of hitmaking. It can't have been because the hit parade wasn't ready for religion, because also in the charts that week was future primary school assembly hymn favourite *Morning Has Broken*. For a man enthused by the power of Christ to save us all, this must have seemed like rejection. Because, despite a phenomenal Hank Marvin guitar line, it flopped and it was a rejection: Cliff released *Jesus* and wept. But when there was only one set of footprints in the sand, Birmingham was ready to carry Cliff.

And we were ready to lift him, right to the top of Alpha Tower. *Take Me High* was Cliff's last film, he was to change from the young heartthrob and, in 1973, redevelopment was all around the town too. Huge modernist blocks sitting side-by-side with the last bits of canal-dwelling culture.

Film Cliff wants everyone involved to join the band. He wants to hastily arrange a parade down Corporation Street. He wants us all to meet at the ramp.

While Birmingham is on screen a fair bit these days, it wasn't then: and to have a film that acknowledged it was set in the city was special. This one literally sung loudly from the rooftops about it.

Slade in Flame starts in the Midlands — although not

filmed here — but as soon as Flame (the band Slade are playing) get success they are off to London. *Privilege*, the third in this sort-of-trilogy of Brum-pop films of the 70s is a dark counterpoint to *Take Me High* starring John Paul Jones as a popstar puppet of the regime in an Anglican-fascist Britain. It's filmed in the Town Hall and even at St Andrews, but it isn't 'Brum', it's another dystopia. *Take Me High* was both filmed and set in a particular Brum bursting with the sort of confidence that only big new buildings replacing slums and bomb sites can provide.

Take Me High is the Birmingham that we want to tell ourselves we were: in our history there's no gap between the Lunar Society, Cliff's Brum, and then the modern gleaming shopping centre we became in the 21st century. 'Forward', the film cried.

It was also so forward-looking that the soundtrack contained a joke about artisan street food being 'the biggest load of bull you'll ever get', something we failed to learn from. The ironists took hold and you can now of course buy a BrumBurger at any number of 'fairs' and 'dining experiences' in the city. In my head the BrumBurger has protected geographical status, like Cornish pasties, or cheddar: to be a real BrumBurger it has to be fried within the sound of someone rattling on about the 11 route, otherwise it's just a generic metropolitan meat patty.

Despite all this, the film entered an almost Schrödingerian state of being forgotten and remembered at the same time. To start with it was really buried, talked about only wherever oddballs with an interest in local history met, but then like everything else it was remembered as something that is forgotten — the internet doesn't mean that there's no right to forget, but that everything is forgotten until it's the right time for a local newspaper website to run a nostalgia feature. Do you remember things? Yes. And when I remember Cliff I'm happy.

Cliff really was trying to save us, and never more so than when he wanted to give us hope in a new millennium — and this made Cliff stand out from his contemporaries. Did Adam Faith try to save Manchester? Did Billy Fury decide to devote his time to letting us know that it was in fact Bournemouth that was a wondrous place? Was Joe Brown always going on about London? Yes, but that wasn't the point. Cliff was rejuvenated by Birmingham and was ready to return the favour many times over.

An eternal flame, lit as a torch by the now Sir Cliff for world peace at the start of the millennium, sat on top of a huge metal globe in Centenary Square. The Flame of Hope was the idea of a group of churches across the city, but it was clear that no-one involved in planning the flame had ever lived in a house where you had to think about whether you could afford to put the immersion on.

British Gas sent an estimated bill for £12,000 a year and when the meter was finally read the bill was red too and the council turned it off.

"Obviously it was not for an eternity, we realised it had a lifespan but it was something other than just the excitement and dreams of one year," said Reverend Mark Fisher, from Birmingham Churches Together who had put it up. Hope — for the time being — of a better Birmingham seemed extinguished too. But Cliff, of course, wasn't going to take that lying down.

In December 2013 I woke to the clock radio featuring Cliff using Radio 4 programme Saturday Live's feature 'Inheritance tracks' — a mini two-pick *Desert Island Discs* where the notable choose records that mean a lot to them — to send a coded message. He selected what he called "one of the greatest pop-rock songs of all time": his own *Wired for Sound*. You know, the one where the video has him rollerskating round a concrete dream that could be the back of Central Library (it was in fact the centre of Milton Keynes, but we know what Cliff meant).

By going against decorum and tradition, selecting his own record, Cliff was telling us to be more brash and self-confident. He was banging a drum and blowing his own trumpet — both of which are difficult to do on roller skates.

Did we miss the nuance? Was the message more detailed? Should we have been more proud of being a 'concrete city' (as the song *Working* from *Take Me High* called us), or was it about ever moving forward? He liked tall speakers, he liked small speakers — should we have got ex-Blues striker Kevin Francis and R2D2 Kenny Baker to do a joint lecture tour about their home town?

In the build up to the London Olympics, Cliff helped to carry the Olympic torch from Derby to Birmingham as part of the torch relay. This leads me to believe that Cliff wants to burn the city to the ground to cleanse us with fire. That, or he wants to stage the second biggest barbecue in Europe, give you a free burger and then talk to you a little bit about letting Jesus Christ into your life.

As the Commonwealth's ultimate trendy vicar — trying a bit too hard but ultimately well meaning and cool in the way only those that plough their own furrow can be — doesn't Cliff Richards just remind you of Brum and why it's not shit?

JB

Black Mekon

The band Black Mekon are trouble. A problem wrapped in a mystery, encased in a riddle, held in a closed fist. There are many theories about who they are and where they come from. Are they the last dregs of the children of missionaries dumped on the Mekong Delta? They certainly sound like bastards from the wrong side of the river. Or are they an alien virus made flesh? I'm sure they wouldn't mind being described as a sonic disease. Or are they avenging noise gods? It's hard to tell.

Their gigs are spores that grow out of nowhere in the forgotten parts of the city, damp rituals of sweat and abandon. Pinholes of chaos that pierce the woven vale of order and normality with prayers a minute and a half of disorder long.

Birmingham has some terrific bands who I love dearly. Table Scraps deliver grinding oil-stained garage fuzz rock, Total Luck are relatively new but deliver the sort of shoegaze normally reserved for someone getting their head kicked in, Swampmeat Family Band are Americana covered in Birmingham dirt, and Rotunda are Punk legends still ripping up the dancefloor. Please seek them and give them your support.

But for the sort of intimate sweat soaked thrashing I crave, my first love will be Black Mekon.

Mekon have a small but dedicated following, not just in Birmingham but world wide, yet they choose to make Birmingham their home. Perhaps it makes sense:

Birmingham has an industrial gravel heart, the echoes of its hammers and nightly sirens its own music.

"Promoting in Birmingham is like playing on hard mode." I spoke to Steve, as close to a 'manager' as Black Mekon get and definitely not a dark priest of a forgotten church, no. Anyone that puts events on in Birmingham knows what he means: it's hard to get people to turn up to things here. Steve would know more than most, part of the ColdRice promotions that held gigs in Birmingham no one else would put on. Kid Congo, Soledad Brothers, The Gun Club, Bob Log III, and the fearsome King Brothers all passed through Birmingham thanks to them.

"We often lost money, but it didn't matter, we figured we'd have spent the same travelling down to London to see them anyway." Black Mekon were often the support, that's where Steve gets cagey. Referring to them being part of 'the deal' they made. With whom he refuses to say.

ColdRice developed out of Ramshackle, easily one of the biggest and best indie nights in the country at the time. They were essentially given free reign with the smaller venue next door.

"We saw the little stage and knew we couldn't put full bands on, luckily the sort of music we were into were one-pieces or a couple of people". Steve tells me ColdRice never really wrapped up, it still pops up now and again, more dormant than dead. Black Mekon themselves are producing an album in hibernation.

"They'll be gigging again, I couldn't stop them if I tried."

I've often compared music to magic. I think it's because I wasn't born with even a scrap of a musical sinew so seeing musicians perform, to me, is witchcraft. The skill of producing something musical is so far out of my understanding it appears magical. But I've developed my thinking on this, a skill is a skill and musicians work hard to develop these skills. It's almost insulting to pass them off as otherworldly and by extension, unearned. But there is magic in music and Black Mekon demonstrate it better than most.

The alchemy is in taking a beat, a few chords, and vocals, all deceptively simple, and transforming them into an energy, a force that binds the audience and artist together. The magic is moving people to dance, to forget who they are for a few minutes, to share a small sacred moment together, unguarded and raw. That is true magic.

And if I sound like a fan, that's because I am. When did being a fan of something become 'uncool' or embarrassing? Fuck that and…

Fuck Black Mekon, I love them.

DS

Digbeth

If you want to be arch, and I usually do, it's really easy to dismiss Digbeth.

As you walk down from the shops of New Street's Grand Central and the Bullring, the very safe and commercial environment soon gives way to more downtrodden streets. Go deeper still and the graffiti gets thicker — and better, too. You realise that many of the warehouses are in fact bars and venues, or work spaces full of freelance graphic designers, or sometimes all of those things at once.

As you make this walk it's easy to read Digbeth as a wannabe Shoreditch or a poundshop St Pauli and to fall upon *Nathan Barley* references to explain it all away. Keep that feeling to one side. Keep walking. Soon you reach the heart of it all: the Custard Factory, spilling out from under the viaduct.

It's harder and harder these days to find the edges of the Custard Factory. Sure, there's a building, a parcel of land, that is the legal entity "The Custard Factory", but it's hard to know where the Custard Factory proper ends and the next plot starts — the gravity of its vibe is immense and very few of us can, or would even want to, really understand the business affairs of the Gray family to unravel it all.

The Grays are a cabal of property svengalis who oversee much of Floodgate and Milk Streets, and whose influence spirals out from the Custard Factory — a seed that they planted in 1992. Bennie Gray is the patriarch of the family, and history will almost certainly remember him as the guy who made Digbeth what it is today. In fairness it's probably true. He wasn't the only person to spot that the cheap properties in Digbeth could be turned into slightly more expensive properties that would attract young creative businesses, but he was the only one who stood across from the coach station and blew his own trumpet.

The web companies, graphic designers and filmmakers that Benny Gray coaxed into units at the Custard Factory brought daytime footfall to an area that was a mix of low density residential and taxi repair body shops. It also kept people there after the office closed, served by bars, cafes, and warehouse clubs. Despite all of this, famously, the area didn't get a cash point until long past the point where everyone paid for everything by card.

There was always a Digbeth before cool-Digbeth. In the vernacular of our city-planners Digbeth is also the Irish Quarter, and still is, but in the marketing of the city Digbeth isn't "A Hundred Thousand Welcomes" from the Irish community: it's a craft beer, a graffiti walk, and something artisanal for your tea.

Here's the sort of typical marketing bumf people conjure up to describe Digbeth now:

> *Once-gritty Digbeth is a developing, bohemian district known for street art like the curved JFK memorial mosaic. A young, hip crowd attends events and creative workshops at the Custard Factory and Eastside Projects, and heads to concerts at the O2 Institute and grungy clubs in former warehouses. Digbeth Dining Club is a weekend street-food*

market with global dishes, and Victorian-era Irish pubs dot the area.

And that still sounds like it could be pretty exhaustingly trendy, yet weirdly it's not. It's actually pretty great, in spite of the enthusiastic but vacant PR twaddle constantly spun about it.

So much of Digbeth is totally inexplicable to me, but I can't help look at it and feel glad that they're doing it. For example, I used to go to a barber's in the Custard Factory. They took over the little glass box that used to be the home of Rhubarb Radio. It was pretty cool. Nice guys. Nice vibes. Somehow they scaled up and took over a nightclub size venue next door. They now do haircuts and food and drink and club nights. This makes no sense to me, but it's going great. Fair play, Stag Barbers. Fair play, Digbeth. This is bonkers and it's terrific.

But that's not all.

In Digbeth they have a Peaky Blinders festival (of course they bloody well do) and they've got an indoor adults-only crazy golf where one of the holes requires you to avoid multiple dildos. Its venues have hosted an interactive screening of *Showgirls*, *Citizen Kane* performed as a series of tweets, and a podcast festival in which the headliners served a made up sci-fi cocktail and inexplicably mimed playing the keytar for five minutes. It looked good on the tape.

They had a blue plaque commemorating a bloke from D:Ream playing in a puddle (it wasn't Brian Cox or the singer, one of the other ones). Meanwhile a local arts space hosted a deeply twisted village fete, the radio station ran a show that did Christmas in August (complete with a fake Noel Edmonds who woke up a nice man from Moseley and dragged him to the studio to get a present). For reasons that barely made sense in 2009, there was a tech festival that tried to run alongside the internationally renowned SxSW in Austin, Texas (which was sort of a joke, but was it a joke though?).

Digbeth has the oldest pub in Birmingham, but it'll send street food to your table via a QR code. And they have a table tennis pub: the most Methodist church youth club activity of them all, but it's in a pub.

How does any of this work?

Yeah, it's easy to be cynical about a cool kids playground like Digbeth, where every surface is a canvas for graffiti, where grown-ups will scooter to work without irony, and where it feels perfectly OK to sell vintage Apple Macs, but it'll charm you and I promise you it will impress every visitor you take there.

It probably works in the end because it's in Birmingham. Nobody is trying too hard, and the stakes are pretty low because nobody expects anything to be that cool, everyone just has a go, and it all somehow works. And everyone is happy too: Bennie and the other Grays can blow the trumpets (the rest of us won't), breathless PRs can gush about how edgy it all is, and the rest of us can just grab a cocktail (possibly blow off the hair if we've just had a trim), pick up a paddle, watch out for the dildos and just have a good craic.

JH

The Villa and The Blues

I've held Villa and Blues season tickets. I've been to Wembley with Villa and to Cardiff with Blues. I was there on the last day of the Holte End terrace and when a thrown pool ball (a stripe, if memory serves) whistled past Gary McAlister's head as he took a corner in front of the Kop/Tilton corner. Essentially, born within spitting distance of the Trinity Road stand, I supported Villa until my late teens, although I went to the odd Blues game — standing on the Spion Kop watching dreadful Birmingham teams heading to the old third division.

Then, without going into too much detail, one of my best mates, a bluenose, died and when I came out of the funk around that I was all in for the blue boys. It felt right. My dad was a Blues fan who'd been to St Andrew's school and lived right by the ground, and I wanted to please him. Blues were the underdogs, and I felt like one. More than that, there was one thing that really worked for me with football: 'Shit on the Villa' was such a great song.

I have a European Cup Final-attending, Steve Hunt-worshipping, Cowans-bothering uncle who, after a beer or two, will happily launch into SOTV. I've heard it sung on the beaches of Europe and in the bars of New York. I've had times of falling out of love with football, but never that song.

I very rarely watch the Premier League because top-flight league football is broken, lasting not much more than a hundred years since Villa helped invent it. Global capitalism has ruined what hooliganism and local capitalism couldn't. Never has a football league been named more oxymoronically than the proposed 'Super League', except perhaps the Evo-Stik League that is paradoxically split apart into Northern and Southern sections.

If you've watched a top Premier League match in the last few years on the telly, you'll have noticed that it looked not like football did: but something more pristine? Perfect grass, shining at you in the right colour, the crowd static, the players all so universally healthy and the play so universally quick that the speed of the game is uniform and therefore appears slow to the viewer. Every game has the lustre of a meaningless pre-season friendly in the sun.

But Villa against Blues is different. Not only are both clubs comic in their own way, the rivalry is a world away from the religious intolerance of Glasgow or the bored banter of Manchester. Jonathan Liew, then Chief Sports Writer for The Independent, called it right: "the Second City derby is one perhaps best characterised by a glorious, gleeful pettiness".

It's not to say that it doesn't get physical, on or off the pitch. The Battle of Rocky Lane is perhaps the biggest example of violence of recent years.

Early evening in September 2002, 150 Aston Villa fans fought around 50 Birmingham City lads to celebrate the teams' first meeting in the Premier League. They fought across waste ground and dual carriageways, with fists and knives, with drainpipes and bottles, with each other and with police.

"Yet again Blues had to bring it to them despite the game being at St Andrew's. They were the ones that were tooled up. They had bottles, knives, gas, bricks and sticks and they go on because one of our lot had a piece of car engine. If you watch the video [of it] you can hear the bottles landing before you see any of them. […] There were thirty of us against 150 and they call it a result as we didn't turn them over — judge it for yourself."

This quote from 'Wally' is from Caroline Gall's book *Zulus — Black, White and Blue: The Story of The Zulu Warriors Football Firm.* The book itself is uncritical, trading tabloid outrage for access to the leaders and organisers of the gang. It's part of a trend that came before hooliganism's recent revival — a rewriting of the 80s that longs for an era grounded in working class life so much that it's willing to overlook assault, battery and Sergio Tacchini.

But this is not the reality of the rivalry. From years of going to games, I only felt real trouble once, and not in Brum. In Toulouse during the World Cup 1998, after a disappointing England loss, the town and the atmosphere turned dark. There had been trouble with the locals before the previous game and all the bars were shut. Trudging across the shiny cobbles we were joined by a group of lads we didn't know. They were scared and wanted us to walk with them as they got to where they had parked. They had seen and heard of people being attacked, both by Toulouse's finest, looking for a scrap, and also by a group of Birmingham City fans who were taking out their frustration on other England fans: and they were hunting for Villa.

I was with a couple of Villa fans, an Albion fan and two Liverpool fans. We weren't scared exactly, but this was something to keep out of the way of. Feeling oddly vulnerable in shorts and T-shirts as dark gathered, we quickened our step and eventually dropped the lads at their vehicle. It rattled round the tiled wall of the car park... "Shiiiit on the Villa" and you could hear bottles being smashed. At that moment it sounded menacing, and eerie, but still incredibly funny.

Shit on the Villa — like most football chants — is based on a popular song. *Roll Out the Barrel*, or more properly *The Beer Barrel Polka*, was written by Jaromír Vejvoda in 1927 in what was then Czechoslovakia, and the occupation of the country by Nazi Germany may have helped it spread, as Czechs emigrated.

Apparently, Sir Edward Elgar came up with the first football chant in 1898. He — a Worcestershire lad who had worked playing violin in William Stockley's Orchestra in Brum for nearly 10 years — would read in the papers about Wolverhampton Wanderers' striker Billy Malpass. One report described the way Malpass had "banged the leather for goal" in a match against Stoke City. Elgar was inspired, and he set it to a short piece of piano music called *He Banged The Leather For Goal*.

In his book *We Lose Every Week: The History Of Football Chanting*, Andrew Lawn quotes the British folk singer Martin Carthy as describing football chants as "the one surviving embodiment of an organic living folk tradition." But football chants, as opposed to cheering or community singing, didn't really catch on until the 60s. By then, Birmingham had adopted and bastardised Harry Lauder's *Keep Right On*, which can illustrate Carthy's point well. Even in the version sung by Blues it has oddly deep and complex lyrics, but it doesn't speak to rivalry, and worse it doesn't address the lion in the room.

Before too long though, Blues fans would have Shit on the Villa, and a real meme would be born. It really is very catchy, Coventry fans sing it, Albion fans also on occasion (even though no-one in Brum cares). But once I swear I heard it on radio commentary of a Norwich/Ipswich derby in the early 90s. That could be the mind playing tricks: when I hear *Roll Out The Barrel* I hear Shit on the Villa. Why is Liberace playing it, why is Chico Marx playing it in *A Night in Casablanca*, why can you hear it in the BBC footage of the VE Day celebrations? Because they're a load of shiiiite?

Is it the simplicity? Shit on The Villa only has 11 words, repeated in not-that various combinations, or 12 if you count 'shit' and an elongated 'shi-i-ite' as separate. That's 10 more than 'boing boing baggies baggies' and 11 more than 'vil-la' as chanted from the Holte End, but Birmingham City fans have always been the intellectual ones in the city. Villa don't really have a come-back that works, even if they try.

The reason that 'Shit on the City' as a retort from them doesn't make the grade is because it's just not clear what the Villa fans want to shit on: no-one ever thinks that blues have an issue with the Roman remains at Bays Meadow near Droitwich.

You can tell if someone is Blues or Villa just by looking at them, fans, that is, not usually players, but sometimes a fan becomes a player and that elevates them. Paul Tait — a Blues player from Sutton Coldfield — represents to me the Platonic ideal of a Blues fan. Scoring the first ever 'golden goal' (briefly teams won if they scored the first goal in extra time) at Wembley in the 1995 Football League Trophy Final, he ran to the fans, took his shirt off and revealed he was wearing a T-shirt underneath. It had a drawing of the Blues mascot, bulldog, Beau Brummie and the legend 'Birmingham City — Shit on the Villa'. Two weeks' wages as a fine seems a small price for him to pay for the most delightful piece of that "gleeful pettiness".

Over 20 years pass and the fashion for the hairstyle 'curtains' comes round again, and with it the polar opposite to Paul Tait: Jack Grealish. Grealish looks and feels like a Villa fan. There's just something about the way he walks, the confidence in his dribbling, the way he falls. During Euro 2020 as he became the darling of England supporters, his Brummie accent was often giggled about on social media: in part because it's possible to hear it without the sound turned on due to the way his mouth forms around our rounded vowels. When you actually hear him speak, with trained Brum ears, it's clear he's a posher lad from Solihull.

Early 2000s proto-Grealish, Lee Hendrie, ended up playing Sunday League football with Blues contemporary Paul Devlin, and there's no real reason to suspect that many Blues or Villa fans can't hang out together, even the really hardcore. But isn't this all just a 'feeling' and is it really special in any way? I feel it is:

no other local rivalry can swing from hatred to gentle piss-taking so quickly. Very few others feel like this, and I think research can prove it.

There isn't too much academic literature on Blues and Villa fans, except Adam Benkwitz's 2013 PhD thesis (*Clashing Sub-Cultures: The Rivalry between the Fans of Aston Villa and Birmingham City Football Club*), in it there are a wealth of interviews with supporters, including this one from 'Archie':

"I remember another occasion, it was 1982 Boxing Day at the 'Sty', oops I mean St Andrew's. Villa were European champions, I was with my friend, we were with our girlfriends in the day, up town before the game and we both went our separate ways to support our teams. I remember him asking me where I was meeting other people, I said I can't remember the name of the pub, because I thought he would come with the Acocks Green crew to have a go. The pub was the Forge Tavern on Heath Mill Lane. The point here is although I know I would not have been attacked by my friend it just goes to show the mentality between the two sets of fans i.e. huge hatred then friends again afterwards. I still don't get it after all these years."

Benkwitz also identifies a difference in "the Birmingham football rivalry" as opposed to others "specifically, themes relating to perceived class and socio-economic status and the history of the two clubs": by which he means Villa fans are all rich and from Sutton. Or rather he means that that's what I would say, because it's what we think rather than the truth. Liew in The Independent says "this is not a rivalry based on religion, or politics, or class, even if Birmingham fans like to deride Villa as the club of Prince William and David Cameron and the establishment".

Liew goes on to hypothesise that the divide is based on turf loyalties between criminal gangs such as the Peaky Blinders and the Whitehouse Street Gang in the late 19th century being absorbed, over the first half of the 20th century, into the city's football culture. Like most things talked about the Peaky Blinders it's probably nonsense, and that's part of the joy of Blues against Villa rivalry: it's based on pretty much nothing however we intellectualise it.

It's a deeply felt cultural identity that can be switched off at the drop of a hat; razor blade in it or not. We care, until it doesn't matter. But when we care we are gloriously petty: and that's the way it should be.

JB

That Photo of Bill Clinton at The Malt House

As photos of middle-aged men still in their work clothes having a swift half after a meeting go, it's a pretty iconic one.

The thumbs up from the balcony, staring down the barrel of the camera, the slightly fuzzy smile that speaks of being three-pints-deep in the sun or the disconnect of being the President of America and still having to have a packet of scratchings for tea. You don't need to look at it, you can imagine it, but if you do look at it you don't see Bill Clinton outside a pub, you see the essence of what Birmingham in the late 90s was.

Only a few days previously the NIA had held the Eurovision Song Contest. On TV, Terry Wogan's intro was accompanied by a tracking shot fading from old canal footage, it zoomed under the Tap and Spile and into the bright sun reflected off the featureless glass of the ICC. Fireworks were set off dangerously close to the Forward statue, and Wogan complained that he'd had to give up his hotel room for Clinton.

That week, and the G8 summit of 1998 was a fulcrum on which Birmingham tried to turn its image. Not to improve itself per se, but to look like it was: to the extent that the council sprayed dead grass next to the Coventry Road on the way from the airport green rather than replant it. Bill Clinton and Tony Blair, with their third way, were painting neoliberalism green and hoping we didn't notice that capitalism was dead underneath.

We have it on good authority that his security detail destroyed the glass Clinton used, to stop any genetic information that could be useful falling into the wrong hands. It seems overkill: as we learned later in the impeachment trial, he was not that fussed about where he left his DNA.

Birmingham, after Clinton left, destroyed any semblance of cool about the pubs by the canals, turning them into an identikit group of chain outlets, focus-grouped out of existence. The Clinton photo was the height of Birmingham's attempt at waterside culture, the G8 supposedly a revival of Birmingham's fortune, but all it ushered in was a boom in stock photography of people laughing alone with salad.

"It's really nice now, round by the canals," people were conditioned into telling each other by constant publicity, and when Birmingham wanted to market itself it was keen to show a broadsheet journalist or a style magazine photographer just how many young, expensively clothed, mainly white people could stand in the sun near a small body of water.

Come, have a drink in an untucked shirt — as long as it's ironed — don't worry, if you get a taxi in and out you may be able to fool yourself you aren't in Brum at all. Birmingham really leaned into the 'more canals than Venice' line at this point, while doing its best to make them seem more banal too.

In a way this was a trial run for how the town would 'pivot to retail' upon the opening of the new Bull Ring in 2003. It was only because they couldn't that they didn't plaster our minds with photos of George W. Bush trying to go the wrong way up one of the escalators. Birmingham is always looking for a new image, and will cling onto the cocktails of any famous person having a drink, Lady Gaga in the Prince of Wales (yes, apparently), Gwen Stefani at Bassetts Pole (no doubt), and you can still panic the staff in the Pitcher and Piano by dressing in a suit and telling them Putin's popping in for a pint.

Clinton, a man for whom surface was everything, would of course find a pub where he could look like a man of the people; but be separated by what essentially was a moat from those people.

At the time my sister was working at The Trocadero on Temple Street, she told me that the day after that 'a load of foreign men in suits' came in, followed by a bloke who she was told later was the then Russian President Boris Yeltsin. He apparently had a glass of vodka and then left. There is no evidence of this, as Yeltsin of course did not tell the press, and it probably isn't true: but I like to believe it anyway. Maybe Germany's Chancellor Helmut Kohl ended up at The Ship Ashore before legging it over to Snobs, Jacques Chirac trying to get the wink about the lock-in at The Ben Johnson.

Where else did Clinton go? Did he pop to Mr Egg, back when it was good? Did he choose the classic rock room at Edward's No 8? Did he take an intern to Rackhams and splash out on a dress? Nah, he had a pint of Brew XI and went back to his hotel: even world leaders can't get a decent pint half the time, and the egalitarianism of Birmingham there should make you proud.

JB

The Flapper

The Flapper opens in 20 minutes and the crowd is bubbling. So much so that they're breaking the years-old English tradition of ignoring each other even if the person next to you is on fire. It'd be disconcerting anywhere else but The Flapper is special. The people here are a mish-mash of ages, colours, and shapes. One thing unites them — none of them fit inside the narrow purview of social expectation.

Back when Birmingham City Council wasn't quite so broke, every so often they would pay a firm to rebrand Birmingham as a city. This would normally involve long lingering shots of the same couple of square miles of the city centre, and pushing our canal network as some cosmopolitan utopia of outdoor cafes and people somehow jogging and smiling at the same time. This was a situation so removed from reality they might as well have shown a samurai surfing on a dolphin while drinking a chair. The smiling joggers are the opposite of the crowd waiting today.

Lumps, bumps, crutches, an old boy in a wheelchair, girls with short hair, boys with long hair, tattoos and even a goth or two. The misfit majority. I see friends shaking hands, saying, 'how do you do?'. They're really saying 'I love you'. Rock pubs are the drip trays where the overflow is collected, where you go if you don't quite fit into the standard serving.

There were about twenty people when I first arrived; closer to double that when they came out to open the gates 10 minutes later. The crowd applauded and cheered. The weirdos rarely win, except when we do.

The concrete pub The Longboat was built in the 60s, it changed to The Flapper & Firkin in 93 when taken over by the Firkin brand aimed at students and younger drinkers. In 2007 it was taken over by the current management and kept the name that everybody had been calling it for years anyway.

In the spring of 2017 they signed a new five-year lease, but less than a year later it was announced that The Flapper would close and the area would be redeveloped into flats. A petition reached 12,000 signatures and local residents, loyal regulars, and anyone with a heart dug into the plans and found the flaws. The council rejected the planning permission. After a short extension, the owners closed the pub anyway. Beloved buildings that stand in the way of redevelopment have a habit of mysteriously catching fire in Birmingham, so it is perhaps a surprise that it is reopening today: two planning permission rejections, a global pandemic, and a flammable fallow period later.

The future of The Flapper isn't clear, the most recent threat being 45 flats proposed nearby. But if its history is anything to go by it'll go down swinging.

It's hard to tell exactly how many people are here until I relocate to the last empty table outside. The soothing shadows and largely guitar-based soundtrack replaced by the sun, tempered by the canal's breeze and 20 or so group conversations. I don't know these people, but I know these people. The Flapper is for them, just as it is for me, one of a precious handful of places where we can drink and relax without the weight of the glances and stares of others.

I don't know why we were walking along the canal, perhaps we were going to or from the Science Museum that used to be on the fringes of the Jewellery Quarter. I know I was ten because the teacher with the class in my memory is Mr Goode. I looked across the canal and there was a building with a funny crane, loud music and I could see lights flashing in the small windows. To my young eyes it looked like a cross between a theme park and an arcade. ADHD heaven. I now know that it was The Flapper, and it was by far the most interesting thing I would experience all day, including having swear words whispered to me through a giant cone from the other side of the room or a sort of rainbow refracted through a grubby quartz block.

"Can we go there?" I asked Mr Goode. He smiled a grown up smile. I don't remember what he said next, something like, "Not today," or even a wistful, "It'd be nice", but I remember that smile. That I-bet-you-fucking-do-out-of-everyone-here-of-course-it-was-you smile.

And he was right, me and The Flapper now go way back with stories that flatter neither party but are cherished nonetheless. I've seen countless gigs downstairs in the tiny black cave of a stage. Watched many friends' first tentative steps into the music world, but also bigger names — not that they were big at the time. Birmingham needs venues like this, small sweating boxes that turn burgeoning bands into gods and stars.

I've spent long summer nights in the beer garden,

concrete still warm from the heat of the day, chatting to strangers, laughing at nothing, grateful for this oasis just a flicked cigarette away from the desert of banality and casual aggression of Broad Street.

My favourite thing about the place is that special time of day in the summer; just before the sun actually sets but when it has disappeared behind the buildings that surround it. The conversation drops a little as the whole outside area glows from the light bouncing off the canal and windows nearby. At that moment that beer garden could rival anywhere in the country, or world, for that connection to a place, that feeling you get when you and the spirit loci dance, and that singing second where you and home meet.

DS

Centre for Contemporary Cultural Studies

Who are you, then?

I bet you can't tell me, or at least you can't with any consistency because who we are, or rather who we tell people we are, shifts based on context.

We all have multiple identities. They overlap, and they conflict with one another, some can dominate, while others remain mostly hidden, and each is revealed in turn as we play out our roles and enact ourselves in any given moment. And every time we make a choice, we tell a story about power and control, and our place within their structures. I know this because I am, or was[1], a member of an academic tradition which grew from the work of English Literature and Sociology academics in Birmingham.

The Centre for Contemporary Cultural Studies (CCCS) was founded in 1964 at Birmingham University. Until its closure in 2002, CCCS was central to the development of Cultural Studies (often called British Cultural Studies), which in turn gave the world the theoretical aspects of what is now called Media Studies.

Initially led by Richard Hoggart and Stuart Hall (the good one[2]), the early work of CCCS was described as multi-disciplinary or even anti-disciplinary, and so it remains a little bit difficult to define what cultural studies is. In this regard, cultural studies is a little like art or porn: you'll know it when you see it.

CCCS's work was essentially a (post)-Marxist project that explored identity, race and class in contemporary British life and had an interest in how media and cultural work shaped and was shaped by these ideas. CCCS broke ground on the theory of what we would now think of as sub-cultures and developed many of the approaches used to study popular culture audiences and 'texts' (in media studies, any artefact is a text even if it's a radio show, movie or computer game).

Peel back most of the ways that we talk today about fandom, you'll find a straight line to the work of the CCCS. Contemporary ideas about identity? The CCCS is in the thick of that. And any time a right-wing mouthpiece dismisses a critique as being "from the woke left", they've almost certainly been annihilated by an argument founded in cultural studies.

So who are you, then? If you're reading this you almost certainly have a pinch of Brummie in you. Whether you live here now, or have in the past, Birmingham is one of the ideas you can pull on to explain yourself to the world. What's interesting, from a cultural studies point of view, is when you might choose to bring your Brumminess to the fore (and when you might play it down). For example I'm known amongst friends and family for having something of a chameleon accent, which can run the gamut of non-geographic public school to some bloke you had a drink with in Perry Barr before the Villa game. Guess which one comes out when I speak to the bank, and which one gets an airing when I buy a second-hand car.

And what does it mean to be a Brummie anyway?

Londoners negotiate their rights to belong through the soundscape of their districts: born within Bow Bell's peel and you're a bona fide cockney, anywhere else you're just mockney. Northerners can define themselves by pies and places named after cakes but if you weren't at the Sex Pistols gig at the Free Trade Hall then you're not from Manchester (which is OK as pretty much everyone was there).

These are complex rules and systems, and we distrust them. Of course we do, for we are BRUMMIES. And what defines us? It's not space, time, or seminal music experiences. It's wanting to be here or from here.

Siôn Simon, erstwhile politician of these shores, once said:

> *It is the best kind of club: something that is worth being part of, which anyone who wants to can join, just by wishing it.*

> *If you feel you belong here, you're a Brummie. If you're proud of this place, with all its kinks and wrinkles, you're a Brummie. If you want to be a Brummie, you are. It's a simple as that.*

You can be a Brummie if you want to be. You can be Malala, born and shot in Pakistan, but the quintessential Brummie. You can be from Kiddy and pass it off. You can be Stuart Hall of Kingston or Richard Hoggart of Leeds and just move here and write the book on this stuff. You can be what you want to be. Revel in your Brumminess. It's not shit. It's delightful.

JH

1   See what I did there?

2   This is one of our six or seven jokes, see also Taking Someone Up The Ackers. There were two Stuart Halls who rose to prominence during the 60s and 70s — one was a Jamaican born public intellectual and Marxist (the good one) the other was a royal knockout nonce.

Taking Someone Up The Ackers

'Up the Ackers' is our favourite joke. Well, our favourite that can be written down: it's no photo of Sir Albert Bore.

Without lifting the curtain to show you how the sausage is made, we often talk about 'only having four jokes' which we repeat depending on the circumstances. Like the difference between the Palisades and the Pavilions, the actual number of jokes we have we can't be bothered to count. There's the existence and photos of ex-council leader Sir Albert Bore, the lack of ladders that once afflicted the new library, and Andy Street's lack of action on his priority of dealing with homelessness. Now Sir Albert Bore definitely exists, the ladders were once missing although we have to assume they may have popped to Wickes's by now, and we don't know what Andy Street is up to: he's blocked us for pointing out he's a Tory.

So that's three. We have more than we thought, although now we examine them they have dodgier foundations than those that stopped Birmingham having a tube. Some had tiny or no basis in fact: we've made the gag up and run it into the ground; lighting up the Library in different colours, celebrities on the quiz machine in the Bull Ring Tavern, and the Service Birmingham Capita contract being 'found' (it was never lost, only hidden, but the 'finding' is the better joke). But those are gags we've forced, repeated until they become funny (at least to us), and they exist only in our world.

What eventually makes them amusing is the shared knowledge, the access to our little club, which exists within the city but separate from it.

'Up the Ackers' is a special one, because it doesn't even need the knowledge that we've done the gag before, it only needs the shared knowledge of the city. As a joke it's a little bit like how visiting stand-up comedians do something about Mr Egg, but good. And like Snobs' carpet we're sticking to it.

This sort of hyperlocal gag is a joy, an unmitigated delight of our shared culture. They are inconsequential but warm and beautiful like a scallop eaten on the way home with the family's chips. The best walk home is of course, from Dad's Lane chippy, down Dogpoo Lane.

The Ackers is a dry ski-slope and activity centre in Sparkbrook, it is a charity and has provided outdoor 'adventurous' activities for Brummies — often in school or youth groups —. since the early 80s, it's also a brilliantly 'hyperlocal' euphemism. It's properly, now, called 'The Ackers Adventure' which is a whole other and more detailed chapter of the story.

You can get too niche, but there are other gags that work on a city-wide basis. Some are funnier than others, but often take place up Bournville boulevard. Outside that bodily area, I love the gag 'Jesus loves you, everyone else thinks you're up Clent.' but there are so few opportunities to use it. To that end, I've written a new joke:

One Villa fan to another:

- Where did you take the missus for her anniversary?

- Upper Doug Ellis

For Blues fans this can be recast as 'Upper Tilton', although this doesn't work as well as it is often not open due to structural issues, and when it is, it can be given over to away fans.

And if you fancy using it yourself, here's a related follow up North Stand? Not since Brian Little left, etc. (Blues fans replace Main Stand and Trevor Francis, Albion fans weep into your beatbox routine of 70s and 80s managers' first names, Don, John, Ron, John, Ron, Ron, Ron, John, Nobby, Ron, and Ron, Walsall? Nice meat van at the market, staffed by Elvis.)

In his book *Jokes and Their Relation to the Unconscious* Sigmund Freud suggests that "our enjoyment of the joke" indicates what is being repressed in usual serious talk. I like to think that our delight in the clubbish nature of our local gags is about moments of acknowledgement of our shared reality, a real connection in a world where so much is mediated for us. If HSBC want to produce a localised 'Brummie' mural on the side of a pub they can play with 'cobs', 'Mr Egg' and the word 'bostin' (never used anything but ironically) but they'll never get to our soul.

The way to the heart of England is through a euphemism for sticking something up a back passage. Up our culture, up our city and up, up, up our Brum.

JB

The Battle of Saltley Gate

Close the Gates! Pete Jackson's pamphlet about the 1972 Battle of Saltley Gate contains the words "and the defeat of the Tories" in the subtitle, but it's clear looking at the state of the nation that if we won the battle, we didn't win the war.

Britain's miners were struggling for a decent wage, and their leaders — including a young Arthur Scargill — were getting on top. The practise of sending pickets around the country to agitate and back up local strikers (known as 'flying pickets', they were later outlawed as an industrial practise and moved on to terrify people with their acapella renditions of pop songs) was leading to glowing support and a solid strike. The winter was cold and the lack of coal was starting to burn, or rather not, as there were possibilities of power cuts.

The West Midlands Gas Board had a huge store of coke in Saltley, which is odd as it's usually kept in footballers' houses in Sutton. But it was crucial to the government in keeping the lights on and breaking the strike. There were over 100,000 tons of coke, and around a thousand lorries a day going in to collect: if the miners could stop the distribution here they would go close to winning the dispute. The local Transport and General Workers Union were picketing, and throwing their lunchtime meat pies at the lorries, but the numbers weren't there: they needed a mass of local support.

The call for solidarity picketing at Saltley gates significantly raised the stakes for all workers in the city.

Anyone who has ever been at a meeting knows how hard it is to get anything done, but this wasn't about which agile project management system to use, or what colour the website should be: left wing political meetings are filled with people with actual ideological positions and deep knowledge of praxis, who may also have petty factional disagreements based on what colour the logo should be (red, obviously).

The feeling then was strong. Arthur Scargill appeared at a meeting of the East Birmingham district committee of the AUEW engineering union. There he said that he didn't just want collections of money for the miners, he wanted Birmingham workers to come down to Saltley gates and stop the lorries leaving with the scab coke. "If they wanted to give us a quid to ease their conscience, then stuff it," he said later.

'Close the Gates' was the slogan, and workers from all around the city were ready to strike in solidarity and march to the battle. Thousands of workers began to pour into the area around the coke depot. Until then the police had managed to get it all their own way, forming a barrier against the pickets to allow the lorries access.

Scargill describes the tense wait, the streets were eerily empty and nothing moved until "…over the hill came a banner".

"As far as the eye could see it was just a mass of people marching towards Saltley. There was a huge roar and from the other side of the hill they were coming the other way. They were coming from five directions…"

Bill Mullins, a shop steward at the Rover Solihull

Plant, said, "It is difficult to say how many were there but the police later estimated 15,000. The anti-union Birmingham Evening Mail that night said at least 10,000. I and many others thought it was a lot more than either of these figures."

"Certainly at least 50,000 workers came out on strike that day, of course not all going down to the picket line."

"The cops knew then they were beat and with Scargill, who by now had got up onto a public toilet roof 50 yards from the gates, encouraging the mass ranks of workers forward, the Birmingham chief constable ordered the gates shut and the lorries turned around."

"A huge cheer went up from the mass ranks of picketers with this victory. It was undoubtedly the most significant moment of the strike and a massive victory for workers' solidarity."

Arthur Harper, President of the East District of the AUEW, reported that the Deputy Chief Constable of Birmingham said, "Arthur, I've only got a couple of hundred police and you've got 10,000 men here on strike. You've got the whip hand today but remember this, I can have 20,000 policemen here tomorrow". Arthur said, "Remember this, Deputy Chief Constable, you get 20,000 police here tomorrow, I'll get 200,000 pickets."

Reginald Maudling, the Home Secretary, later wrote "Some of my colleagues asked me afterwards, why hadn't I sent in troops… And I remember asking them one simple question: 'if they had been sent in, should they have gone in with their rifles loaded or unloaded?' Either course could have been disastrous."

Thousands and thousands of Brummies had downed tools and marched to Saltley, held firm and closed the gates, and beaten the Tory government and the establishment.

Birmingham felt more militant afterwards. Harper thanked the miners for bringing disparate parts of Brum's trade unions together, "the miners did us a good turn in Birmingham that day, 'cos they united the trade union movement of Birmingham, of all trade unions, that's been falling out with one another and this day, they united Birmingham".

Not long after, the King Kong statue in Manzoni Gardens was occupied by two flying pickets protesting about low wages in the building industry as part of the national builders' strike. They sat on his shoulders and hung a banner round his neck: "King Kong says nothing less than £30 for 35 hours". Class war was spilling out to gorilla war.

Shop floor militancy was at its height in the early 70s, and we're all well versed in the stories of the stoppages at Longbridge and how they supposedly led to Thatcherism as a change that was needed. "It's that Red Robbo from The Leyland's fault, Stew," as they say, they being essentially the right wing. This includes Thatcher herself who called him a "notorious agitator". But the story is not often told from the worker's perspective.

The 1972 miners' strike doesn't get the historical

coverage of the 1984-5 one, and that's for one simple reason: in 1972 the working class won. A couple of years later following another stoppage, Prime Minister Ted Heath called an election and asked 'who runs the country, the government or the miner?" Heath lost.

For a time, the working class won the battles: we won in Birmingham. That it was thanks of solidarity across the working class, across industries and across geography, makes me proud.

JB

Calling Roundabouts 'Islands'

The council tried to get us interested in 'circuses', but we persisted.

You want more? First, perhaps, I should let you in on the fact that outside Birmingham people don't call the circular road junctions where people give way to the right and move clockwise to an exit 'islands'. No, in the rest of the UK they are referred to as 'roundabouts' and in the US they are referred to as 'the work of Marxist Devils' due to the inherent co-operation and equality without signal control they suggest.

We in Birmingham like traffic islands, we like things that go round and round: the 11 bus, the Superprix and the cycle of underinvestment and having to knock down and rebuild buildings in the city centre.

Think of those islands and the feelings their names produce: the Swan Island, the Pagoda Island, the Spitfire Island. You can picture not only all three as places in Birmingham, but their fantasy versions based on the name. The Swan Island a prelapsarian idyll or a place where Gulliver gets his arm broken on his travels. The Pagoda Island a quiet contemplative temple, an oasis in the blur of the modern world. The Spitfire Island a giant poppy, simultaneously an act of remembrance and a place of conflict, especially where the lanes merge going down to the M6.

Think even of 'Buffet Island' which isn't the name of the island, isn't one singular place, and in the case of the one that used to be The Navigation on the Tyburn

Road, isn't even on an island. It isn't a South Seas paradise awash with gala pie and bowls of nuts, but that's pretty much what you think of. That they haven't opened a patisserie version called 'Dessert Island' is everything that's wrong with capitalism today. But the visions, it's the word 'island' that does it: giving most people a thought of a desert island paradise in the middle of the road.

For me the thought of an island is based around the comic strip *Desert Island Dick* which used to appear in The Topper (a DC Thompson sub-Beano, sub-Dandy and even sub-Beezer weekly). Dick lived on a desert island, no more than a mound of sand: like a knee in the bath, with a palm tree on it. He dressed in ragged trousers and shirt, had straggly hair and beard — he'd been shipwrecked at some unspecified time — he was alone and bored, and wanting to escape. At least those teenagers skateboarding under the A38 on the island by the fire station had each other.

I'll admit that the view of a cartoon desert island, the Robinson Crusoe island, the Tom Hanks 'alone with only a signed '82 European Cup winning team signed ball for company' island, is struggling for primacy in our culture. It hangs on out of time, like warehousemen on TV wearing brown coats, and handcarts on railways (for more of these see *Bounds's Dictionary of Memetic Cultural Reference Points*) and for some the only thing keeping it hanging on is the Radio 4 programme *Desert Island Discs*.

If you've not heard it, *Desert Island Discs* is a weekly show, where establishment figures are given a platform to get the softest interview possible. If you have, you'll agree that the best bit is the chance to judge people's cultural choices: are you enough of a liar to pick pieces of classical music, do you genuinely think *That Simply The Best* is the best?, have you picked *Mr Blue Sky* (and if you haven't, you're wrong).

If I'm caught in traffic, I may finish musing on my record selection and move on to lining up my desert island desert islands, The Swan, The Spitfire, Robin Hood Island (which distributes cars from the rich of Solihull into Acock's Green). If I'm ever caught in Traffic, I hope to get Steve Winwood to confirm that *Here We Go Round the Mulberry Bush* is about them going round the island past the Rotunda in the 60s wondering about going into the pub.

We Brummies are an island race, wistful and whimsical in the face of traffic as of much else.

Not a Churchillian 'Island Race', those odd ideas of British exceptionalism and steadfastness, not Del Boy Trotter getting all patriotic on a fishing boat while going to Hull and back "This island race, this septic isle, yeah us Brits we've got salt water running through our veins. When you think about all the British heroes that have set sail out of these waters, to discover the new world… and stitch the dagoes up. Makes you feel very very proud."

Mike Skinner of West Heath and The Streets has said many great things in his lyrics. On his 2021 LP *The Streets* (confusingly not by The Streets, but his other project The Darker the Shadow the Brighter the Light) he tells us "when you love a city, it don't love you back", he's also told us about the hazy fog over the Bull Ring, but when he quoted Churchill with his single 'If you're going through hell, keep going" he wasn't doing much but offering advice about going round The Queensway in gridlock, no matter how proud the paint job makes you of your city. He's telling you to get through and get to the freedom of the next island. Islands define our worldview and build our head cannon of Birmingham as an exotic other.

Circuses are something completely different. And roundabouts make you feel sick. All hail the island as the linguistic escape of the Brummie navigator.

JB

Big Wednesday at Snobs

Snobs opened in 1972, and I'm told, for a while, it was a club in the strictest sense that everyone had to be a member or guest and required a tie and jacket for the men. In 1993 it introduced Big Wednesday, with dirt-cheap drinks and a music policy of indie nonsense or 60s chewing gum. It quickly became a Birmingham institution and rite of passage. If you've ever trod that tightrope of being a certain type of teenager/young adult in Birmingham (indie, essentially, with all perceptible male, white, post-16 educated leanings that means), you've been to Snobs and have a story or two. The really interesting thing is that they are almost all the same story.

One of the reasons for Snobs's endurance could be that the Snobs experience is universal and consistent. Students thirty years ago are able to relate to students even today. Snobs could possibly be a fixed point in time, there has only ever been, and will be one Snobs night. A moment so powerful, even a change of venue couldn't break the spell. All the stories, all the joy, the dirt, all your favorite memories happen on the same night, the same night. An eternal Wednesday, The Biggest Wednesday.

Wednesday is key. For a start there is very little competition. But more importantly Wednesday is a self-selecting crowd. The type of person who can happily, at best, gamble being conscious enough to get stuff done on Thursday and, at worst, barely thinks of Thursday at all because consequences are for other people. All of them, in the only place that's open.

It's worth mentioning the music policy, for nearly thirty years it seems the music policy hasn't changed, more than the music policy, the playlist has barely altered.

> *When he saw me arrive, the DJ used to play Stephen 'Tin Tin' Duffy's Kiss Me, straight away, it was as though he was letting everyone know I'd arrived. I checked with my friend to make sure this had really happened and not just my imagination. It had, maybe because I used to ask for it all night, and this way he got one play out of the way.*

The indie played at Snobs is a stone soup of songs from throughout the years: every generation, maybe one or two songs will permanently filter onto the canon of music. Always the most shout along jump-up-and-down mainstream indie, and then at some point Lee Dorsey's *Working in the Coal Mine*. The gestalt assessing each song and discarding those that work the least. Almost a Darwinian race of new mutations and keeping only what works best.

The night starts with the bouncers who are, let's face it, wildly inconsistent, seemingly letting people in or turning them away based on the whims and fancies of the fates.

> *Taking the belt off my dress to create a tie so some random guy could pass the dress code entry requirement*

Then, well not always then, but it'd happen at some point, one of your crew would fall down the stairs in the ragdoll way only drunk people can walk away from, luckily landing in a crush of people, with the crowd's soft bit cushioning the fall. As you chase your friend cartwheeling down the stairs you take a second to marvel at the wall of faces, what are they? Why are they? Are they trapped souls? Victims, the spirit loci of the building itself pushing themselves into physical space to escape the four thousandth rendition of *Place Your Hands* by Reef? Best not to dwell.

> *One fine night in Snobs, I was on the dancefloor when The Prodigy's Firestarter came on. My mate was getting well into it and waving his arms about, when he swiped the specs from my face.*

The bar will be packed and usually serving in a Lord of the Flies system of whoever is the most obnoxious goes first. They'll be serving drinks so cheap it's more expensive somehow to stay sober; litres of rough, no-brand vodka stripping throats raw for pennies. Every couple of minutes friends come back from the bar with armfuls of spirits.

> *The bars have run out of Jack Daniels for my coke, the barman tries to convince me that Bells is the same.*

It's hard to overstate how crushingly packed Snobs is, the dance floor is soaking wet from either spilled drinks or the sweat you can see running freely down the mirrors that surround you, tiny cubes of glass crunch underfoot as you have no choice but to jump and fight your way through the night, occasionally stopping to strip your vocal chords some more by howling the words with the rest of the wolves.

Towards the end of the 90s I once shook my money maker next to one of the poles, then in a moment of what can only be described as idiot-juice inspired lunacy... I licked it...

Even at the tender age of 19 (-ish — they all do blur into one) I knew I'd done something terrible. As it was, I just spent the night feeling a bit grubby. These days I would have been straight to hospital ordering a surgical scrub of my tongue and a stomach pump so powerful it would have felt like a pressure wash of my hoop.

Those needing a break could escape to the next room via a mirrored passageway, a corridor no more than ten foot long with mirrors either side, that through the prism of dirt grain alcohol will become trickier than a room in the crystal maze. For fun the floor is an ice rink, and the whole experience is akin to a slapstick version of the climax of *Enter The Dragon*.

I always bump into my mate Weird Bob. Bob isn't that weird but he does like the nickname. However when I introduce him as 'Weird Bob' he says: "Robert, Weird Robert". We share a round of vodka shots and he leans in, making himself hoarse as he slowly enunciates a story about his mum meeting her relative at a gathering:

So my mum says "How's your son, what's he doing now?"

And the response is: "He's in the new Star Wars film." (Bob's cousin is Liam Neeson, he does look a bit like him.) "What's your son doing now?"

"He photocopies things."

The 60s room is funkier and normally less busy, its back seats dotted with people getting off with each other, the dark corners hiding eager boys rubbing at denim like they were boy scouts trying to start campfires on girls' labias.

> *I remember losing my glasses in the mosh pit and crawling around on my hands and knees in the near-dark trying to find them without being trampled on because good mosh pits like the one at Snobs are usually very safe.*

You can spend the night in the back room, only venturing into the mass of arms and screaming thirsty mouths of the main room to go to the toilet because the back room toilets are always flooded.

> *Kicked out without any of my belongings (coat, keys, wallet, cash etc), had to walk home to Selly Oak in the cold. Luckily, thanks to my precautionary imbibing, even that ordeal couldn't sober me up.*

You will be sick, no one can throw that much near raw ethanol into themselves without your body objecting to literal poison.

> *I was once sick on a man's arm. He didn't even notice.*

But the choice is go home, or go harder, or go unconscious. I mean it's inevitable that all three will happen, you just have to decide in which order you do it.

> *She bought me a drink, and herself a flavoured spirit of some kind. I asked what it tasted like she pressed her lips on mine and her tongue into my mouth. It tasted good. We went through the tunnel to the small room and danced.*

And then he attacked, from behind me and swinging punches. Her boyfriend. I couldn't hit back, bottle in one hand the other arm in a sling with a busted collarbone. So I tried to embrace him as a tired boxer would do, but as I did I thought 'fuck it' and bit him on the back of the neck. He exploded, but just before he really landed, bouncers thundered over from the front of the dancefloor. Scooping him up in one movement and chucking him out. "You can't attack a guy with a broken arm."

The drink is cheap, yes, but drinking it is not easy. There was a trend to get around the taste by by-passing the taste buds, and the mouth, snorting the neat vodka off the back of your hand, the crook of your thumb and forefinger. You might not have got much down you, but 99% of all known germs on your skin there were dead: the rest were too pissed to do any damage.

In the mosh pit, some guy shouted out "I've dropped a contact!" and everyone moshing got on their hands and knees to help him find it.

The night is truly magical. Magical in that not only is it authentically non-changing in reality, but also is preserved across the generations and tribes in the shared ideaspace. And because of that we can all be young at the same time. It's more than nostalgia, it's an affection and a lifeline thrown across the years that can bind us together.

The DJ in the main room ended with the theme from The Littlest Hobo as the lights went up.

Snobs is egalitarian in its own way, affordable, very little dress code, accepting of everyone. But that's the point ultimately, the drinking, the dancing, the music, the moments on the dancefloor where the ego melts away and by losing yourself in the heat and the exhaustion you all get to be part of something bigger, you get to, even for a minute, see god. Not God, Christian God, but an older god, Dionysus, passion and feeling flowing from the music through you all, connecting you on the other side of thought. Gods are eternal and when we connect to them, we are connecting to, not only each other, but also ourselves in moments before and past in the same state. We live forever in those moments of sweat and joy.

And, of course, the ritual atoning for the sins, the hangover pilgrimage back to Snobs the next day to pick up your coat you forgot about at the cloakroom or the keys/dignity/virginity you lost at some point in the night.

As we get older we dismiss this, we forget, our priorities change, Thursdays start to mean more and our energy becomes alarmingly finite. But forever is still there, next Wednesday on the dancefloor.

I kissed her on the steps at the side of the main dancefloor, I can't remember what was playing. We'd been out drinking for hours after work and had ended up just the two of us wandering around the place oblivious to everyone else. The place was silent and light as I drew back and said: "I love you, you know."

"I know." she said.

Reader, some 11 years later, I married her.

DS

Mr Egg

Mr Egg is not what it was, or rather it never was what we thought it was. The idea of Mr Egg and the reality have just drifted further apart.

Cooking eggs is not as easy as it looks, and this is why, for a post-pub eatery, Mr Egg could not be beat. Or the reason for its popularity might just have been being the only place open at 2am where you could sit in relative comfort and eat what passed for food. When it closed, it was — not to go into the acid detail — because you just could not get the staff. Not ones that hadn't just been convicted of assault with vinegar, anyway.

But who is Mr Egg? It's an identity that is a closely guarded secret, like that of Big John, King Kebab, or those people who post lots on Twitter in defence of Northfield Tory MP Gary 'Big Dinners' Sambrook but about very little else. I decided to crack the case, then couldn't be arsed to ask anyone, and will just do a quick yolk.

I know it wasn't the Marquis de Condorcet, who, during the French Revolution, like a Queen, lost his head and made a huge mistake. Escaping the terror in disguise he entered a tavern in a small village, and blew his cover when he called for an omelette. "How many eggs in your omelette?" asked the innkeeper. "A dozen." "What is your trade?" "A carpenter." "Carpenters have not hands like these, and do not ask for a dozen eggs in an omelette." Seems he didn't realise that one egg would have been un oeuf. Despite Mr Egg's publicity, very few members of the aristocracy are that au fait with egg-based dining.

Brummies were devastated when Mr Egg closed, as were the Glee Club's roster of touring comedians who now had to agree on another local reference to drop into their sets, but in a way I was elated. Mr Egg became pure at that point, transitioning it to what it really was — a meme — unspoiled by anything real that could leave a bad taste in the mouth. But eventually, this is Birmingham of course, commerce prevailed, the meme was poached and a new Mr Egg, smaller, worse, was born. Awful news, but as Second World War winner Joseph Stalin said, you can't make an omelette into street food without breaking eggs.

Things that Brummies love are always split in two: Central Library during its demolition, the 11 route during the Commonwealth Games roadworks championship event and — like the brooms in *The Sorcerer's Apprentice*, each one smaller than the last but still operating independently — UB40. That happened to Mr Egg too: it split, half in Selly Oak, and half in Hurst Street. Literally: the original reduced to 50% of the footprint, signage by necessity removed, legend scrambled. Was anyone surprised? Will the two halves ever be reconciled? You can't put Humpty together again, even if all the men and horses can eat like a King for a quid.

And if that made you smile, I can guess why: one of the only bits of the real Mr Egg in the shared idea of Mr Egg is how great it was when they changed the sign cheekily from 'Eat Like A King' to 'Eat Like A Queen' as the area was designated the Gay Village. There was something perfect in that understated Brummie humour, and I bet they didn't issue a press release.

In the film Sunset Boulevard, faded movie star Norma Desmond says "I am big. It's the pictures that got small." Mr Egg is still big, it's the Hurst Street takeaway that got small, and our Mr Egg — the one in our heads — is cracking.

JB

Perry Barr Cars

My father would get a Christmas card every year from the mainly Muslim staff of Perry Barr Cars, which he would put on the mantlepiece with the others. Twice a week and for special occasions he would ring them, they would get him back home safe from the social club and wait until he'd got the door open before leaving. They looked after him and waited, I like to think, out of a sense of care and community, and not just because they needed to make sure he really lived there so they could come back the next day when he was sober and get the money.

My dad was so loved, that this would be taken advantage of. Unable to get a taxi home from town, my mate Clive would ring Perry Barr and ask for a cab for 'Mr Bounds' and they would venture south into the city centre, even though it was out of their way, to pick up their friend. When Clive opened the door he would tell the driver that 'Mr Bounds' had wandered off drunk and then get a ride back. "Been busy?" he might say, knowing they had been busy attempting to take care of their own.

Jon Hickman, my co-author, tells me that Perry Barr Cars' number was the one he used to give to girls he didn't want to speak to back when he was single (and to be frank, a bit of a shit). At least when those girls rang 356 1818 they would get through to someone happy to pick them up and take them where they wanted. "What time do you get off?" someone would say, if this was a Carry On film.

Jon now uses it on registration forms for websites, to get access to demos and the like, when he doesn't want to be contacted by salespeople. This is why Perry Barr Cars has such a great website.

Before the days of taxi apps, everyone had a minicab firm and this was mine. Becoming a regular you would get to know the drivers, feel warm in their company, their furry seat covers and their overly-heated Datsuns. The air would be heavy with a sense of belonging, as well as Magic Tree air freshener. You'd get a feel of a community cohering, and going in the right direction, probably for around a quid a mile.

How much do you usually pay for that?

JB

Our Relationship to the Sea

I've been to Weston. I'm not convinced.

My Brummie friends think it's ace. They think it's the seaside. And they do like to be beside the seaside, beside the sea, besides the fact it's rubbish.

Look, I grew up on an island and I've been spoiled, I get it, but your bar could be higher than this. Just because it's close doesn't mean you have to go. If you went to things just because they were nearby you'd go to Coventry but you don't because it's like someone took the worst bits of Birmingham and did them on the cheap.

When people find out I come from the Channel Islands they usually ask me "what on Earth are you doing in Birmingham?" And then they go on to point out that I'm as far from the sea as I can possibly be. It's a fair comment.

Landlocked as she is, though, Birmingham has an enduring and endearing fascination with the sea. Many years ago, Jake Oldershaw (a member of Stan's Cafe) interviewed me as part of a project that celebrated the relationship that Brummies have with the sea. He collected stories from people who kept pictures of the sea in their homes and offices, asking them why they would choose to sit in Birmingham and think about the sea. That project, *Midland Aquaphiliacs* has all but ebbed away from memory, leaving very little upon the shores of the internet, but at the time he collected dozens

of stories and photographs from his subjects, and a
surprising number of them weren't even about Weston.

Around that time I remember seeing the Evening Mail
splashing a big story on the A-boards outside all the
newsagents. "Tragedy of Local Sailor", the posters said,
and all I could imagine was a plucky young lad, a head
full of dreams of working his way up from cabin boy to
admiral, stuck staring forlornly at a canal full of trolleys.
A tragedy indeed.

Later I'd learn that Birmingham, against all logic, has a
naval training centre named HMS Forward, and one of
my local scouting groups is actually designated the 1st
Sutton Coldfield Sea Scouts (I can only assume, they're
the first and last). I've seen RNLI flag days raking
it in on New Street ("well they do have a lifeboat in
Weston, you know," a friend told me). Meanwhile, Jon
B swears he has sunbathed on a beach under Spaghetti
Junction and one of the first (and best) viral videos from
Birmingham was *Brummie Baywatch*, in which a lad sits
on a ladder in the Floozie's own jacuzzi, looking out for
trouble in nothing but his boxers.

I find this all endlessly endearing, but I can't help
myself from wondering what on earth is going on,
really, with this draw toward the sea. I guess you always
want what you don't have, so while we love our city
we fancy a bit of the other too. Humans have a deep
connection to the sea, of course, so perhaps that's why
the Brummie race memory has space within it for the
call of the ocean (they keep it with the other innate
Birmingham behaviours, right next to the fact that
it's always Rackhams, never House of Fraser). As for
Weston, if it's what you know, then it's easy to see how

you'd romanticise it: sand castles, rock, ice cream and a pier; forty hours every week then a paid vacation on the Weston shoreline must feel like there is a better lifestyle, Birmingham…

I like to think it's all of this and it's something more. Yes it's odd to stand in Victoria Square and pretend it's the sea, and that's the point. 'Beneath the pavement, the beach' is the given translation of a slogan that emerged from the May 1968 protest movement in Paris. The slogan is associated with situationism and is a response to the urban setting, and the officially sanctioned ways of behaving. To bring the beach to Birmingham is deeply absurd and forces us to really confront who we are: *Sous le Spaghetti, la plage!*

JH

Camp Hill Flyover

JG Ballard was famously inspired by The Westway in London, a road he considered central to some dystopian future that we were actually living in. But if you go to London and travel The Westway, you can see that it is nothing more than an extended Perry Barr flyover — and has absolutely nothing on the wonder that is our very own Spaghetti Junction. Ballard's *Concrete Island* doesn't even have a beach.

But if you like your driving urban, elevated, and thrillingly unsafe then Birmingham had something that could help create a thousand unsettling novels. If Digbeth is our Faraway Tree, then the Camp Hill Flyover was our — rattling and juddering — slippery slip, a helter skelter to the Stratford Road, via sheer terror.

That it's no longer there doesn't diminish how great it makes me feel about Birmingham, our ingenuity, our stoic acceptance of genuinely odd things, and our haphazard approach to the past: we bulldoze that which would be a permanent monument and leave up a temporary flyover for decades. Looking back from thirty years hence feels like turning around backwards — pre seatbelts — on the rear seat of a green mark one escort: the exhilaration is in remembering it. In saying:

"Holy shit, we really drove over that."

Barely as wide as a double decker bus, in fact some types of Birmingham buses were not allowed to use it as it was too dangerous, the Camp Hill flyover helped ease a traffic pinch-point where the Coventry Road hit town.

As you can tell by looking at any single photo, it was prefabricated. Built in Bristol by a firm called Gardiners, they first assembled it in a field to test it. It then spent a while lying behind Garrison Lane tip.

It was installed on one October weekend in 1961, not by specialised contractors but by 'the army'. At least according to the sort of people who live in Thailand, post on local history forums on the internet, and say "I will never return, being no great fan of 'Diversity'".

And nor can we return to those days: the painful nostalgia of pining for something that was genuinely a bit shit is enough. Not too long before it was removed, in 1989, is where I can place my one memory of going over the flyover, on the way to watch my dad play football in the Birmingham Works League on a Saturday lunchtime. His teammate's car took aim at the small gap and powered up and over the hump, the tops of the terraces of shops flashing past. Memories aren't impermeable and the mounting of the flyover now plays to me as an echo of the scene in *The Italian Job* where the minis speed into the back of the coach.

The Italian Job was made in 1968. Had the writers been over the Camp Hill flyover, and based the action on the skill needed to quickly get to anywhere in Sparkhill? Did I really see King Kong on the way past, or had he long gone? We need to be comfortable and celebrate our imperfect recollections suffused with pop culture, let ourselves love our Birmingham not some official record lest, like a terrified driver going up to Camp Hill Circus, we meet ourselves coming up the wrong way.

JB

The Big Heart of Birmingham

In the book *Heart of Darkness*, the lead character travels up the Congo River, looking for an ivory trader supposedly 'gone native'. The book is an examination of place and how people can have an effect on a place and how it can affect them in return. Inspired by this I decided to find the heart of where I live, and have lived more than anywhere else.

I did find the heart of Birmingham, its spiritual centre. The source from which everything springs, the heart of, if not darkness then, the wonderful concrete greyness that everybody seems to be ashamed of.

Not its actual centre, I found that too and it was disappointing to say the least.

But every journey starts with a single step so I started there.

I read somewhere that you calculate the exact centre of a place by cutting out its shape and balancing that shape on a pin. The best photo of the boundary of Birmingham I can find is a heat map from a couple of years ago of the Birmingham chlamydia problem. It was published by the Birmingham Mail website. The Evening Mail started life as an institution made to inform and enrich the citizens of Birmingham, and has now turned into an ugly practically-unusable SEO click-generating nonsense machine, but it's so good at its job of jumping up the Google rankings that a simple search for 'Birmingham maps' spits out a breathlessly tabloid bit of clickbait about the city's clammiest genitals.

After printing and gluing this map to stiff card, I spent half an hour getting it to balance. A task that seems easy before you start, then near impossible while you're actually doing it. But it happens, I push the map down and the pin emerges through the bottom corner of Nechells, apparently a pretty serious 2020 chlamydia hotspot. It's near enough exactly where I make out Duddeston train Station to be.

To get to the train station I get the bus, this seems counterintuitive but I like buses, a quirk of growing up in Northfield where the train station is so far away from where you live you end up adding more time to the journey and you might as well sit in the traffic of the Bristol Road. Plus the journey back from the train station is up several steep hills and it's simply not worth packing the sherpas and climbing gear to get back.

So a bus to town. In town I go to New Street to jump the one stop to Duddeston. Briefly I nip into WHSmith's for a drink, walking down an aisle of magazines and I'm taken back to being a teenager, something about the smell, and the layout. I'm a teenager shoplifting books in John Menzies to pay for tonight's drinks in The Foundry, or I'm just using the shop as a shortcut to bypass the ticket barriers, or killing time before we hide in the toilets to get to Glastonbury. I mentally map the space, and it seems that the entire shop is in exactly the same place as it used to be, a newsagent being the rock on which the whole Grand Central development revolves.

Live in a place long enough and everywhere is strung with nostalgia land mines, ghost traps.

New Street itself could lay claim to being the middle of the city, the transportation hub from and to which all tracks lead. But maybe not, its rebranding into Grand Central has turned it into a bland everywhere. Another 'landmark' barely discernible from any of the others in Europe. It's distasteful to me to have a commercial privately owned space be the heart of Birmingham, which honestly discounts more and more of the city centre every year.

Duddeston is a nothing, barely a station, one platform, no barrier, housing to the East, industrial park to the West. Opposite there's a row of shops with three newsagents, a Dixy Chicken, a hairdresser's and a bookie's. Around the corner there's a mosque centre, and a small brown box called Church of Christ, presumably as in 'Christ! I hope I don't have chlamydia'. But nothing of any note. There's a hole in the exact centre of Birmingham.

But the heart of something isn't the exact physical middle, otherwise people like me would be waxing lyrical about finding a place's lower intestine. It makes sense that Birmingham's heart is in the city centre.

What about Victoria Square? Not a bad contender, the imposing neoclassical council house and town hall with a stern Queen Victoria herself looking on. Dominating the middle is Dhruva Mistry's *The River*, but only really known locally as 'the floozie in the jacuzzi' a name which is not only not accurate since 2013 when repairs to the water system became too expensive, but stolen from the nickname for the Dublin sculpture *Anna Livia Plurabelle*. The Dublin statue is also known as 'the whore in the sewer' which to make rhyme you have to say in the local accent, much like Shakespeare, bab.

The artist won't talk about what the fountain is about but his insistence of the addition of the two towers *Objects (variations)* either side of the statue makes me think of their importance to the piece. For me, when thought about from above the whole thing looks like a uterus with the two *Objects (variations)* as ovaries, which puts the floozie and the main pool right in the womb with the watery steps down into the entrance. I like this interpretation mainly because it puts the lower intestine where the council house is, which makes sense because that's where all the shit collects. Of course this doesn't explain the two sphinxes that flank the whole thing, the *Guardians*. I have great affection for these statues, looking like early Picasso sketches of two butch lesbians from the 80s. If there was any justice these enigmatic creatures would be as iconic as the Bull Ring or the King Kong statue we had for five hot minutes in the 70s. So Victoria Square is a womb, not a heart.

Around the corner is no better, the memorial to Joseph Chamberlain, it used to be a meeting place, where skaters could avoid students coming from the library, and people could have their lunch or just sit and chat. But now it's sterile and anodyne, a corporate architect's wet dream, all character and life jet-washed off and the result sold as office space. All fountains and no pennies, doomed to be photographed over and over, living on social media under the caption 'looking good today Birmingham'. If you're only proud of the same square mile of recently redeveloped city space, you ain't really proud of Birmingham.

A short walk away lies Pigeon Park. One of the things I do love about Pigeon Park is that some of the church officials hate it being called 'Pigeon Park'. One story is a few years ago in a meeting, when a younger member of the meeting called it Pigeon Park one of the elders lost it and compared calling the churchyard 'Pigeon Park' to using the N-word.

Pigeon Park then, is it Birmingham's heart? I don't think so, squeezed between the Colmore Business District and Rackhams feels too out of the way and the cathedral in the centre of the centre doesn't sit right, a building most Brummies haven't been to since the ocean of flowers appeared during the surreal time after Diana died.

My nomination for the spiritual epicentre requires some explaining. Back before mobile phones, and before even pagers. When you said you would meet someone in a place you just had to go. And if you went and they didn't turn up, you just kinda waited some more. Of course you could use a public telephone, if you could remember your friend's telephone number, calling them would just put you through to their mom who would tell you they left an hour ago. Being stood up literally left you just that, standing waiting to see which shoulder deity would win, self-loathing or self-respect? Stay or go?

But where to meet? Ask any Brummie of a certain age where to meet in town and they will, almost by reflex, say either 'the ramp' or 'outside McDonald's on the ramp'. Back in the 90s we called it 'the tramp

ramp' because of the amount of homeless people that would be on it, and because teenagers are hateful little sociopaths until they eventually learn some empathy. The ramp was the perfect meeting place, central with everywhere within a reasonable-ish walking distance, next to the Pavilions but within sight of the Pallasades in case you'd mixed them up, public toilets, and easy sight lines so you don't miss them if they do turn up.

As such it's been burned into generations of Brummies' minds. The ramp is still what most people I know think of when they say 'Town', not the new glass building that could be anywhere, mediated and approved by boards of faceless tasteless bland suits. Dirty, busy, real. Any given day you can stand on the corner of New Street and Corporation Street as people pump past from any direction, free radicals floating through the ventricles of the heart of the big heart of England, feeling the rhythm and beat of Birmingham.

DS

The Reason We Don't Have an Underground

Birmingham is the, wait for it, second largest city in Europe (by population) that doesn't have an underground train system. The largest, Belgrade, has one planned; so at least we'll eventually get to be the biggest at something.

The reasons we don't have an underground are well known: the ground being simultaneously too hard and too soft and wet. The water table is too high and it would cost too much. But these excuses are built on sand, unlike Birmingham which has a good mix of clay and harder rock. We could have had a tube network: but the government lied.

In the early 1950s the Tory government, in a Cold War frenzy, decided it needed to build a series of underground telephone exchanges. Construction of the Anchor exchange — it's pretty much under the BT Tower — started in 1953 with a cover story that a new underground rail network was being built.

Building lasted until 1956 when we were told that the project was no longer viable, but by that time the underground exchange and tunnel system 100 ft below Newhall Street had been completed at a cost of £4 million. It was put under a Government D notice, meaning that even if the press found out they couldn't publish anything.

The main tunnel runs from Anchor to Midland ATE in

Hill Street, from there the tunnel continues under New Street Station and on to the exchange in Essex Street. An uncompleted tunnel heads off towards Hockley and from Hockley back towards the Anchor, but they don't join and there is a gap where this tunnel wasn't finished. If the tunnel had been completed, joining the section coming in the other direction, it would have had a total length of nearly one and a half miles, the gap is just 500 yards. There are other tunnels under our paving stones, such as one from the Mailbox to New Street which had a small mail train running through it.

We could have had a tube. Were it not for the government.

When Wembley was in need of renovation in 2001, the Westminster government decided that £700 million on tarting up North London was better than a brand new £300 million national stadium in the centre of the country by the NEC. Culture Secretary Tessa Jowell gave the London stadium more time to prepare its bid, against the rules of the process, according to the Birmingham team "reneging on its commitment that it would encourage the Football Association to make Birmingham the preferred option if those tests were not met in full". Football could have come home, were it not for the bias of the establishment.

When Birmingham bid for the 1992 Olympics, Thatcher's government would not give it full support. Her decision to maintain sporting links with South Africa in the face of apartheid, which caused many countries to boycott the 1986 Commonwealth Games, was not making international sporting friends easy to come by. Around the same time her reaction to the problems in Handsworth was shockingly dismissive: Oliver Letwin, who would eventually become David Cameron's policy adviser and one of the many problematic right-wing darlings of Remainiac liberals, co-authored a paper saying that "lower-class unemployed white people had lived for years in appalling slums without a breakdown of public order on anything like the present scale" and that funding would create entrepreneurs who would "set up in the disco and drug trade." Further memos to the PM warned against subsidising "Rastafarian arts and crafts workshops".

Since Brum's boom years, the national government has seen the success of the Midlands as damaging to other regions. The Distribution of Industry Act 1945 was intended to stop industrial growth in 'Congested Areas', like Birmingham, and to push industry to declining 'Development Areas' in the North and West. The 1956 West Midlands Plan set Birmingham a 1960 target population far lower than its actual 1951 population — so people would have to leave. In 1964, the government declared Birmingham's growth "threatening", and banned further office development for almost two decades. According to John Myers, who talks of "a plot against Mercia", "the size of a country's cities normally follows a rule called 'Zipf's law', by which the second largest city is half the size of the largest, but Britain is an exception. By one estimate, Birmingham should have twice as many people."

When they decided that the BBC would have to move production out of London, it was pushed to Salford; when Channel 4 was meant to spread out across the nation those ad sales jobs went to Leeds. Much of the prevaricating over HS2 is routinely framed as 'who wants to get to Birmingham quicker', a bias against the city that continues to this day.

Underfunding from central government has been rife in the years of austerity, but larger, left-leaning, metropolitan areas have been the worst hit. Brum lost half of its funding between 2010 and 2020, leading to cuts in already stretched housing and social care services and increased poverty in a place that was already struggling.

Why, then, aren't there calls for Birmingham to gain independence from the Westminster circle jerk? Why did we reject the idea of having our own mayor in not one but two referendums? Why, when a 'Greater Birmingham' (what else is the West Midlands, really?) mayor was foisted upon us, did we not fight harder to get decent candidates elected? How did we let Solihull have the casting vote in installing a weak Tory hanger-on that looks like an air-dried version of Blue Peter's Mark Curry?

The reason we don't have an underground is comic in its dismissal of Birmingham by government. It's one example of a litany of shit, but it *can* instil a sense of pride that we can do without them, that when these politicians come to the ICC on safari once every couple of years, the security they need keeps growing. They try to stop us digging big holes, lest they find themselves down them.

JB

AB Fletcher

There's not a lot they haven't got,

In fact I think they've got the lot,

Who is this of whom you speak,

They're on Dartmouth Middleway, on Great Lister Street.

The home of the motorist, yes you've guessed

AB Fletcher, they're the best.

This is the best I can do at remembering the words of the jingle featured in the AB Fletcher advert screened in the early 90s on Birmingham Cable's L!veTV local opt-outs. The main competing ad featured a (thankfully clothed) toddler sitting on the toilet and shouting "Kav's for Lavs". Both are intrusive memories of the most delightful sort, unresearchable, half there and pointless.

There are others, but AB Fletcher? They're the best.

JB

Lickey Road

"The trick is to pinch them off at the stem just above where they come out of the ground," says Tony. The air is wet and none of us is wearing suitable clothing for the grey sheet of moisture that is passing for weather. He prunes the three or four I spotted after I called him over. We caught the 62 up the hill but they both insisted on getting off early to walk up through Cofton Park so their feet are making squelching noises from sodden trainers. I'm smug in my ex-army boots.

"Also," says Phil a few yards away laying flat on the ground, "don't be afraid to get close to the earth, you can find them faster." I get down and look across at him, ear in the dirt. In between me and him I see four or five crops of the tiny mushrooms, thin with the little nipple at the top.

"He's right, you know," says Tony. I give Tony the 'is he alright?' squint about Phil. "He's fine, probably eating as he picks. Also the stuff in it can be absorbed into the skin so you might get a little buzzed." I take a couple of shrooms from the carrier bag on my wrist and swallow them before I can taste them.

It took a while to work up to it, but now the nightly ritual is to sit on the crest of the hill and pull on my rollerblades. The cushioned insides stink in a comforting way that cuts through the midnight air. The pavement is still warm and my body feels like it's ready to melt into it, which is as much to do with the relief of finishing another 12-hour shift as it is the two or three after-work pints.

Normally I plug in my earphones the first chance I get, but not now. It's not about safety, it's about purity. No distractions. Me and the hill.

I get to my feet, a little push and, BOOM. Warp factor nine.

The hill is unreasonably steep on the path behind the tall hedges. The grass bank between the path and the road is a bruising but safe way to bail if any of the cracks in the pavement take me by surprise. But nothing ever does, at this speed nothing can touch me.

I'm not immortal because I'm young, or because I never get hurt. It doesn't even occur to me that I am actually mortal because I'm not thinking. Not in the moment, I am the moment.

"You alright?" Tony nudges me "You zoned for a bit."

"I'm good." I say, "Where's Phil?"

My pub career is exactly one hour old when my first drunk falls through the door and rolls to the bar like he were on deck of a ship in a squall. I can't understand what he's saying, and in the ten minutes of training that formed a solid part of the hour I've been here, nothing was mentioned about serving people that are incomprehensibly drunk. Luckily the manager, an affable 6'4" alcoholic ex-police officer, tells him flatly to "Get out". Once, twice, then picking him up by the scruff of the neck and pushing him out of the heavy oak door. My manager resumes his position in the bar hatch sipping his half of lager like it wasn't his sixth since I got here.

The drunk guy is banging on the door. Nobody is mentioning it or even moving at all. A couple of old boys are sitting at a far table

*watching the dust mites dance lazily in the beams of light brave
enough to push themselves through the vintage windows. The pub
is a cave, horsehair carpets and thick oak furniture.*

*We hear a crack, presumably one of the small panes of glass on
the door, and the banging stops. I look at the manager, he just
gives me a nod. At this point I don't know if that nod means
'everything's fine' or 'pour me another half'. Later I would learn it's
always the latter. Half an hour passes and I learn the hard way
what a Mickey Mouse is and that you need to take the sprinkler off
the bitter tap if you want to pour one.*

*There's a banging on the door, a policeman's knock. My manager
let them in, but he didn't call them. They ask if a drunk guy
smashed a window and ran away. The manager asks how they
knew. They tell us that when they found him unconscious down
the Lickey Road, they followed the trail of blood back to the pub.*

*After gashing his wrist he must have sat on the picnic table a while
because the pools of blood have already started congealing on the
bow of the table.*

*The pub is a traditional sort, the walls that rough stone render
painted white, so the arterial spurts that gash the walls look even
more vibrant red.*

*"Can you just tidy this up for me?" says the manager to me, while
still talking to the police.*

"How?" I genuinely ask. He shrugs.

"A mop?" he offers, before pouring himself another half.

*My pub career is exactly two hours old and I'm mopping blood off
the walls.*

I tune back in, and Phil is in the middle of lecturing me "...these places are sacred, and everybody has their own spot". I laugh, I don't know why. It just seems so important to him. This is the Lickeys, I grew up around here. Not a secret fairy glade, it's crabgrass two minutes away from a bus terminus' public toilets. I giggle again.

"Do we have to walk?" I moan. I don't mean to, but at 16 it's hard for anything that comes out of your mouth to not sound like a moan.

"Do you good," my nan says, somehow blazing ahead up the hill. My nan is small but radiates the presence of someone much bigger. A car pulls up, a nice one, a very nice one in fact.

"Alright Danny?" shouts Nick as an automatic window slides down.

"Alright Nick." I say. Nick is shifting in his seat.

"You want a lift?" he asks.

"Nah, that's cool, just out with my nan," I say, just as she comes back.

"You both can jump in," smiles Nick. We both know he doesn't own this car, and if I'm perfectly honest I'm not entirely sure he has his driving licence.

"Oh, it'll be alright, I've always wanted a ride in one of these." says Nan as she climbs into the back and introduces herself to Nick. She's beaming. I also get in the back so I can shift my nan over from sitting in the middle of the backseat where she'd be able to spot the screw driver sticking out the ignition. To be fair to Nick he

doesn't belt it up the hill and manages not to stall it. He pulls over smoothly and we climb out.

"You've got nice friends," my nan says approvingly.

"Yeah I do," I confirm. I do have nice friends, Nick isn't one of them.

How did we get here? Phil and I are waiting outside the newsagents. Tony must be inside, since Tony never got out of the habit of not paying for stuff that even Phil left behind in his teenage years. Phil's looking at his nails, like really looking at his nails.

The factories have always been there, impossibly tall churches of oil and dirt, brick and broken glass. The smell of petrol and engine fluid has an indelible connection to the summer as the smell of wet pavement and the air just before a storm.

Most of my family works or have worked there, as do all my friends' parents. Working at Rover didn't seem like an option, it felt inevitable. Some things become just shared knowledge, nights are good money, the first shift are bastards that always steal your tools, and there is a rigid hierarchy of who works on and off the track.

I know that the gantry that connects the two factories either side of the Bristol Road carries car chassis, but I'm still young enough to think that's how Longbridge got its name. Other secrets have to be gleaned, sneaking glances through doors of the machine rooms propped open in the summer or the long broken windows, climbing the fences to glimpse at the deep sepulchred workshops of oily tools and endless racks of strange metal shapes.

I'm at one of the disappointing open days, we've just walked up the infamous Heart Attack Hill, named after some poor sod who couldn't take the exertion of the steep slope that leads up to one of the newer factory buildings, all pastel green corrugated aluminium and swept floors knowing the family would be round on the weekend. My uncle (well, one of the adults in my life who call themselves uncle) nods over to the expanse of finished cars, parked bumper to bumper.

"Want one?" he says.

"Yeah sure," I shoot back, he leans in and makes sure the tour guide is out of earshot.

"The keys are kept in the right headlights, the cover's not screwed in, you could just drive away," he taps his nose. I never do.

We've stopped by the car park of the factory, Phil's having a piss. Tony is trying to get him to do it in a bottle so Phil can drink it. Apparently the psychoactive somethings are filtered through the body and are stronger that way. Phil isn't interested. I'm giggling at the thought.

Noise. Loud noise that you feel as much as hear. The earth growling at my feet. I've pushed my way to the front of the legs and coats. I let out a whoop, but I don't hear my own shout over the noise. I only feel the noise in my throat, so I shout again. Other people are too, I think. The bikes rumble past. I asked earlier why they do this every year. I think someone said something about wearing helmets, but half of the bikers are wearing them and half are not so it's hard to tell if they're for or against it. The smell of exhaust and the endless stream of bikers. Noise and joy.

Traffic noises jolt me, we're at a bus stop. No one likes the vibe of the bus stop so we decide to walk. I cross the road to the central reservation, it's like a different world.

Younger now, not only do the trees shoot up around me, but the adults legs seem just as tall and solid. We're walking on the central reservation, each side flanked by horse chestnut trees. To me it's a yellow and orange tunnel with a canopy filtering the autumn sky like stained glass. I'm collecting conkers which are suddenly the most precious items I own. Dad is throwing sticks into the trees to knock more down. My grandad is ahead with the dog. He seems to like being by himself but smiles patiently when I show him a particularly good conker. My mom and nan are fussing over my brother and sister who walk so slowly as I run and launch myself into the cushion of wet leaves.

DS

Lenny Henry Doing David Bellamy on Tiswas

We dig deep into the undergrowth of popular culture to define ourselves as a city, really get our hands dirty and *grapple me grapenuts* if Lenny Henry's impression of naturalist David Bellamy isn't the best compost to grow a city's identity in.

It's impossible to do an impression of David Bellamy: you can only do an impression of Lenny Henry doing David Bellamy. In the same way, if you try to write about Birmingham as a city you can only write about the impression it has given you. It won't sound much like it, won't look anything like it, and your beard falls off.

Lenny Henry is from Dudley, but Brum has taken him to heart in the same way as we feel ownership over Noddy Holder (Walsall), Julie Walters (Bearwood), and Meera Syal (Wolverhampton). That his major early career successes happened here (winning *New Faces* as well as *Tiswas*), is all we need: and he sounded a little bit like us too.

With Delbert Wilkins he reflected back what we felt about authority and the police, only a couple of years after the Handsworth riots. They were not on our side, no matter how much they would sponsor local football tournaments. I was too young to understand the riots but I knew it was us against them. here were a couple of days of a frisson at school, being sent home early as 'a group of youths have started congregating on the

Lozells Road' and, a few days later, Dad coming home from the pub with a video recorder.

Lenny in recent years has talked a lot about the need for representation at all levels and in front and behind the scenes in the media. In his autobiography he's clear about how his experience of race and racism was shaped by the lack of other black people in showbusiness in the late 70s and early 80s. Seeing that people like you are involved, as well as the actual advantages to culture and equality, is heartening. And Lenny Henry did, I felt, do something for representation of people from the Midlands — Lenny felt so much like one of 'us', an honorary. He was charming, funny and the jokes were from him rather than at him, a rare thing for a Black Country lad.

Another thing that Lenny has told us in recent years is how much he idolised Don Mclean (not that one, the guy from *Crackerjack*) which again feels like a very Birmingham thing to do. Yes, here is a man that has worked with some of the biggest names in comedy, but reserves the highest of praise for someone who is pretty much forgotten outside Brum. When Don McLean (not that one) met Don McLean (that one, the *American Pie* one) backstage at the Moseley Folk Festival Birmingham loved it, but no-one else cared, and that's the beauty of our celebrity parochialism.

Tiswas is revered in the city more, perhaps, than anywhere. It's a Channel 4 'Do you remember things' programme cliché to say that *Tiswas* was a kids' programme that was watched by adults, but that was really true. We were usually not allowed in the front room of our house off Aston Lane where the colour set was, instead relegated to watching TV on the 14-inch black and white portable in the back. But when my Dad got overtime on a Saturday morning at the IMI — time when the management were not there — he started to take the portable in with him to watch Tarrant and the team. So I got to see *Tiswas* in colour, which must have cemented the anarchy and sensory overload in my young brain. In the summer, when Swap Shop or whatever was on, the toolmakers at the IMI had to do something else, and as Dad said "our cars had never been so clean".

Judging by my age I must have come to *Tiswas* just at the time that Lenny joined, and I loved it. I got to sit in the audience once. One of Dad's mates worked for ATV as a despatch rider and snuck me in. I sat just to the side of the 'cage' of grown-ups (mostly students I later learned) that would be pelted with water or shaving foam whenever things got quiet. I was nervous and starstruck and can't remember at all what happened: apart from the fact I was pissed off that I had missed *Tiswas* because I had not seen it on telly.

As Lenny was an impressionist, his broad characters were the bits you could do yourself, along with throwing water and pretending to fling flans (who had shaving foam in the early 80s unless you were a TV star?). If you didn't do the Algernon Winston Spencer Castlereagh Razzmatazz 'ooooooooookkkkkkkkaaaaay' at school and demand to try condensed milk sandwiches, were you really a kid at playtime in Brum?

When the Four Bucketeers later released the *Bucket of Water Song*, I drenched myself on holiday, scooping cold and leaf-strewn swimming pool water out and over my head while singing the chorus over and over again. That the video for the song features the team marching around a fountain by the Hall of Memory in Centenary Square, showing that they couldn't be bothered to scout a location more than a hundred yards from the ATV studios, reveals so much of how it was a homemade enterprise: so much more special to me for being a couple of miles from my home.

The atmosphere of half-rehearsed madness, catchphrases and in-jokes became a template for a certain type of telly that would dominate British TV in the nineties, without it you wouldn't have seen Chris Evans, *Soccer Saturday*, the behind-the-scenes at reality TV 'X-tra' programmes, or and any bit of Russell Brand's early act that didn't directly reference his dinkle.

It's surprising just how little of this brilliant anarchy is in the public domain. *Tiswas* was so huge that it appears that the camera couldn't really capture it; or at least there is no way to package and resell it to us. As Lenny says, "It was like being in The Beatles, a huge fanbase and freedom," though only one hit record.

One bit that survives on YouTube is Lenny bearded-up and doing a 'rural retreat' at a very urban Bellamy's Garage. You can tell that someone from the *Tiswas* team has spotted the place on the way to the studio and made the connection. He drags John Gorman dressed as a comedy native American out of a boot, does a gag about 'windscreen vipers' and has a piggy back from a man in a pig mask down the road past the waste ground to close. It looked very Birmingham. Someone's built plenty of cheap housing (cheap to build, not rent) and, more surprisingly, planted a tree which also obscures the view: but you can see by triangulating from the tower blocks that it's around Granville Street. There's even a Bellamy House around the spot where the garage would have been: it's a shit block of flats. The Premier Inn is only a couple of minutes walk away, which would have been a better tribute.

We built our city on the ruins of Lenny Henry's David Bellamy impression, and that was a really good place to put down roots.

JB

Spotting Birmingham on Telly and Film

Hollywood!

The drama, the glamour of it all!

That's right, I'm talking about the little village, south of the Maypole, whose famous sign pulls people in from the M42 up into Kings Heath and Moseley with promises of gigs at the Hare & Hounds, or a scallop at the Atlantis chippy. Hollywood! A dream factory which brummies know gave the world big stars such as Duran Duran's John Taylor and Arsenal's Alan Smith.

It's fair to say that Hollywood, Worcs. has given the world some of its purest cinematic moments. I think of Hollywood and I immediately think of the most woke and progressive Bond movie yet made — the music video for Duran Duran's *A View to a Kill*. But it is Smith who put the most drama on the village's slate when he starred in the most dramatic football match of all time.

On the final day of the 1988-89 Football League season the top two teams in the league, Arsenal and Liverpool, went head-to-head at Anfield. The teams were so close on points that the outcome of the day would decide the title. Arsenal, who hadn't won the league for 18 years, needed to win the match by two clear goals to take the crown.

Our lad Smith, playing for the Gunners, scored early in the second half, but as the clock ticked down, and without the two-goal margin Arsenal needed, it looked like his effort would count for nothing. That's when it happened. The sort of thing that would only happen in a movie: Michael Thomas broke through with a second goal deep in stoppage time. Liquid cinema.

That match is often seen as a turning point in the football cinematic universe with all of football existing prior to or since that moment. Liverpool-Arsenal 1989 wasn't just a match. It was the culmination of multiple narrative threads, and it set up a massive new arc of storylines: Italia 90, the Premier and Champions Leagues, English football's slow and steady march back toward the top of club football and international relevance (this one is still in production, but we're getting there). Nick Hornby wrote about this moment eloquently in *Fever Pitch*, his autobiographical exploration of football and identity. When the other Hollywood came knocking and asked for a movie of the book of the thirty or so years of hurt, the middle-act magicians of cinematic story-telling could only reproduce a thin simulacrum of those incredible events.

As is their wont, Hollywood, LA, tried again. They rebooted and remade *Fever Pitch* transplanting the action to Boston and replacing football with baseball. The American movie planned a believable and downbeat ending, in which the Boston Red Sox would continue an 86-year wait to be champions. But the magic that started just off the Alcester Road with our own Alan Smith could not be denied and it sprinkled down tinseltown stardust on the baseball field: the Red Sox dramatically won the championship mid-way through filming, forcing a rewritten happy sporting end.

It's a surprise to me, though, that *Fever Pitch* was filmed in Boston at all, when such great tax breaks are available for filmmakers to come to Brum and dress it up as New England.

In the 1970s and 80s Birmingham might occasionally make it to the pictures: Cliff Richard's *Take Me High* told the story of a young man disappointed to be sent to Brum for his work, but who ultimately takes to the city and walks around the centre of town in sequences that defy space and time; *Telly Savalas Looks at Birmingham* was a rose-tinted 80s tour of Kojak's kind of town (he loved it, baby); and on the smaller screen, 70s grimy crime show *Gangsters* did love to film a car chase on the A38 overpass by the fire station.

In more recent years, we have had to make do with seeing Birmingham as a stand-in for other cities as an ever wider network of film and television productions have been drawn to the second city, bringing the likes of Steven Spielberg and Tom Cruise to town. Brummies love this. We love the attention, we love to feel seen by the super famous, and we can't get enough of seeing the photo ops of them outside our balti houses. What we dig the most though is that little shot of recognition we get when we see our places and spaces on the telly and cinema screens. Whether it's pretending to be the Home Counties, Ohio, or Manchester, we just love to nudge each other, point and say "I know that place."

The high point for this call-and-response relationship between brummies and TV was when the BBC show *Hustle* spent three years dressing up the same two or three streets as a sort-of-London. The show became event television for anyone whose aerial pointed toward Sutton Coldfield, as locals would (as the tabloid journalists say) "take to Twitter" to call out every time they saw a place they recognised. Over the years, as the fabric of Twitter has changed, and as more and more shows come to Birmingham, the participatory nature of this has changed a little but we all still surely feel it in our bones, that need to call out every spot you make?

A personal favourite of mine is Birmingham's involvement in the mega-hit bent-coppers show *Line of Duty*. Originally filmed in Birmingham, but set in an unnamed city, production moved to Northern Ireland but brummie DNA endured through the rest of the show's run. In the first two seasons it was possible to play the traditional location bingo (The disused Central Fire Station where they tortured Steve! The stupid two-way escalator at Millennium Point! The police station is Birmingham Municipal Bank at the bottom of Broad Street! Jackie Laverty lives on the Four Oaks estate!!!)— and that was a lot of fun. The later seasons kept their local interest through a new meta-game. Brummie fun came in combing the screen for hints — not clues about who was H, but evidence that we were really in Birmingham still; Brummies were frequently cast as background and supporting characters, and the 0121 dialling code was never hard to spot, but the real delight came in seeing the Sutton Coldfield constituency map still being part of the AC12 'crazy wall' right at the end.

The biggest hits with a local link sometimes seem to duck the city altogether. In the *Harry Potter* movies the Weasley family are shown to be amiable and somewhat goofy Brummies, but the main one is inexplicably from Essex. Tolkien's Middle Earth which stretched from Moseley to the Black Country is now forever Peter

Jackson's and New Zealand's — and we didn't even get the consolation prize of Tolkien's biopic, which was mostly made in the North West, as was much of the quintessential Birmingham representation *Peaky Blinders*.

It is of course disappointing that *Peaky Blinders* seemed to employ more talent from Cheshire than it did from anywhere near the Chester Road. It is also a shame that the first time Birmingham got a chance to shake off being the comic relief character it reveals a dour demeanour with a penchant for a bit of the old ultra-violence. But what this show gives us now is a huge boost of soft power.

Let's call it the Tout Test: when you're walking the seafront in a holiday resort, what are the restaurant touts going to shout at you in the split second they have to build empathy?

"Hey my friend!"

"Where are you from?"

"Birmingham"

"PEAKY BLINDERS yes please my friend come in come in. HA HA HA TOMMY SHELBY yes please AUNT POLLY OK please by the window OK?"

And before you know it you're already a jug of sangria in and he's showing you the photos of when Big Ron ate there in 1993.

But *Peaky Blinders* is worth more to us than just getting a slightly better table in one of thirty indistinguishable restaurants in Málaga. This huge worldwide success has brought Birmingham onto the world stage in a way *Boon* never managed, and it's massively raised the stock of *Blinders* show-runner Steven Knight.

Steven Knight is a proud Brummie and he's keen to share his moment with his city, becoming the frontman in various ways for the city's attempts to encourage yet more filming to come to Birmingham.

There are some who want to bring all the energy around marketing Birmingham as a film location under the umbrella 'Brummiewood' — a very obvious idea that's been knocking around since at least 2004 when a Flash-based website first graced its dot com domain name. There are of course many other 'woods: Nollywood in Nigeria, Ghollywood in Ghana, and Wellywood in Wellington, New Zealand to name a few. Brummiewood sounds a bit naff (and apparently Steven Knight thinks so too) but it could prove useful in getting the less imaginative to send more movies our way, so we should lean into it.

The only question that remains then, is this: if Hollywood brought us the mega-blockbuster, and if Bollywood is the home of fantastic fantasy musicals, what genre can Birmingham make its own?

So far, via *The Girl With All the Gifts* and *Ready Player One* we're doing a steady line in dystopian fables (we even stood in once for apocalyptic Manchester, in the BBC's reboot of *Survivors*).

Wherever Steven Knight takes us, I'll be there next to you squealing every time I see a pub where I've had a beer, cheering for things I know, and telling you "Yeah that's actually an office on Colmore Row though".

And hopefully before too long, Brummiewood will be able to tell its own stories, perhaps the story of a sleepy village on the way down to the motorway, where dreams are made.

JH

Getting Bought Drinks in Perth, Australia

Being from Birmingham, specifically South Birmingham, and very specifically Longbridge-cum-Northfield, got multiple drinks bought for me from strangers in the most remote major city in the world.

I was in Australia, not really doing much. My intent was to travel but with no plan and no discernible skills I was running out of money fast. It's my own fault. As soon as I got off the plane and into a taxi, I had asked the taxi driver to "Take me where the action is." He took me to Kings Cross, or known locally as 'The Cross' which at the time was an area known for its bars, nightclubs, brothels, strip clubs, peep shows, all manner of debauchery, and as luck would have it, cheap accommodation for backpackers. This is where I would spend the next month and the bulk of my budget.

My master plan was to get a job bartending. I spent another chunk of my budget getting qualified as, at the time, working behind a bar required a 'responsibility of serving alcohol' certificate. This was part of a raft of measures including the controversial lockdown laws that would be introduced in later 2014 that saw a lot of the places in Kings Cross close.

But my plan had a flaw. There were plenty of bar jobs going, especially for backpackers and those a little more flexible about being paid unconventionally.

Unfortunately those jobs went to prettier, younger, and distinctly more female applicants.

So running out of cash, and options, I answered an advertisement in the paper about 'making money while traveling the country'. I turned up for a training day, the gig was selling CD-ROMs door to door. Kids, CD-ROMs were basically a CD that could store a whopping 700Mb of data, which does not seem a lot now, but back then computers weren't much more than tin boxes with a couple of calculators gaffa-taped inside, and if they were connected to the internet at all it was by messenger ant. The real challenge was being able to deliver the patter word for word without sputtering in disbelief at the bullshit coming out of your own mouth.

Needless to say I was deemed top of my class, and they flew me to the furthest patch. The team was situated in Kalgoorlie, a mining town with dirt roads, two skimpy bars and a heroin problem. A skimpy bar is a pub with the usual sort of depressing decor and regulars, but made all the more bleak by not letting the bar staff wear more than their swimming costumes to work. I spent two days knocking doors before I quit. Which left me with a problem: still poor, but this time poor in a trailer park in the middle of the fucking outback with no public transport system. I hitchhiked to a coach stop and was able to negotiate myself onto a coach to Perth.

In Perth I got work in the fields and vineyards, my digs were a caravan I shared with an unbearable Canadian. The other workers were one called Figjam (which I was later to learn stands for Fuck I'm Good Just Ask Me), a silent Korean guy who thankfully did all the cooking, and a stoner who more than once locked the shopping and his keys in his car, which I would have to then break into.

Finally with some money in my pocket I got to explore Perth. Perth is just over 2,000 miles away from Sydney; in fact it's easier and cheaper to get to Bali from the cities on the East Coast of Australia than it is to get to Perth. The nearest city with over 100,000 people is Adelaide, more than 1300 miles away.

Which is why when at a bar the first time I was out drinking, I couldn't believe it when I got stopped.

"Excuse me, are you from Birmingham?"

"I mean, yes, that's a good ear, how did you get Birmingham?"

"You sound exactly like me Grandad."

"Do you know where abouts he's from?"

"A place called Longbridge, where they make the cars."

"I'm from Longbridge!"

"Awww mate, strewth! Let me buy you a drink."

(Yes they do speak like that, shut up.)

Once is a coincidence, but it happened again, and again.

After the third time I did some research. In 1945 the Australian government brought in a scheme to replace workers after the war. As part of the deeply racist 'White

Australia Program', they gave workers from Britain and their families passage to Australia for a £10 admin fee, to resettle and fill jobs in the burgeoning manufacturing industries. They targeted people already skilled at working in big factories. Which means a lot of people, when faced with a choice of a life of rain and dogshit of Longbridge, or the beach, left the car plants of Longbridge to start a new life in Perth. These became known as '£10 poms'.

And the South Birmingham accent is so virulent and recognisable that the grandkids of these immigrants could recognise it from across a bar and buy me a drink.

I don't know if I'd still get drinks bought, the first generation of £10 poms must be all but extinct now. But it is good to think that a tiny industrial area of South Birmingham can still exist outside the very niche knowledge base of people who know Birmingham. That even in one of the most remote cities in the world Longbridge is remembered and loved.

DS

Coda

A month after I quit that door to door job I got a call on the burner phone I was using in Australia from the main trainer who I'm not ashamed to say I flirted my heart out with to get the job. She was livid that I'd quit, and told me that I would be reimbursing the cost of the flight and my accommodation (two days in a caravan).

I put the phone in the nearest bin. I didn't even bother to hang up.

Tony Hancock Not Giving a Fuck About Birmingham

"Things just went wrong too many times," has always seemed the ultimate sad end. Sadly it's from Tony Hancock's suicide note rather than the council statement on deciding not to bid for the Olympics for the third time in a row.

The statue of Tony Hancock in the middle of Old Square in town is one of Birmingham's genuinely interesting pieces of public art. The use of space to give the impression of a photograph printed with half-toning echoes how that the square would once have been awash with nicotine-stained journalists from the Post and Mail building that used to throw a shadow there. It's now cracked and tagged, a great piece of street furniture for skateboarding, but unloved by officialdom or capital.

Anthony John Hancock was born in Southam Road, Hall Green, but, from the age of three, he was brought up in Bournemouth and pretty much never gave us a second thought. This would not be unusual, in fact most of us remember virtually nothing of anything that happened before we were three. Infantile amnesia is the inability of adults to retrieve memories of situations or events before the age of two to four years. That there was no attachment to his birthplace at all would seem to indicate that his parents didn't care much for Brum either — they moved for "the good of [his father's] health".

But Tony's performances — embodied by the Anthony Aloysius St John Hancock version of himself: 'the comedian Tony Hancock' — have a great deal to tell us about our attitudes and our city.

The lad himself, Tony's persona, was downtrodden, often conned — mostly by Sid James — like Birmingham, turned over again and again by central government: "Pssst, 'ere mush, wanna bid to be Channel 4 headquarters, only one million nicker? Yak yak yak yak".

In *Sunday Afternoon at Home*, Tony was a slouching, bored figure rattling through a closed world praying for stimulation. This was every Sunday in Birmingham before the late 1990s, and it feels like that at times now too, if you don't think shopping is a leisure activity.

Sunday Afternoon at Home is regarded as a classic, a real leap forward in sitcom. One half of the script writers, with Alan Simpson, Ray Galton said "We just wrote 'pause' in the script and left it to the actors to experiment with how long it could be maintained. In those days, there was nowhere to go, nothing to do on wet Sunday afternoons; once you'd read the papers you were stuck: the pubs were shut and the pictures didn't open until about 5pm".

And *The Bowmans episode* explains Brum's *Archers* better than any viewing window into the studio at the Mailbox — curtains closed when recording — ever could. Whatever role TV/radio Tony was in you can paint pretty much anything you want onto the performance of Tony Hancock, providing that ultimately ambition is thwarted. He could play Birmingham in an episode and it would work perfectly.

JB Priestley, writer of *An Inspector Calls*, said of Hancock that he "overdrew on his intellectual bank balance", just the sort of snobbish thing that would be said of Brum. This is then followed in classic broadsheet prose by 'but if you actually go there'… and retrospectives of Hancock do the same.

Later in his career, Hancock co-wrote the film *Punch and Judy Man*, based on his boyhood in Bournemouth. I'm conscious that he never made a film about running the streets of Hall Green or the old Bull Ring, the sort that would have had Brum nostalgia buffs foaming. He often said that he wanted to create a work that would cover the whole of human experience, "from the first plip to the final plop" — but that did not cover large concrete shopping centres, underground pubs or long circular bus routes. He did not look back in love or anger, he did not look back at all. Forward with Hancock.

Despite being one of the first mass-media megastars the UK had seen, the star of the first real British sitcom, the crucible of comedy's Industrial Revolution: he's not majorly feted by the public in the way even the stars of Dad's Army are. That makes the memory of him sweeter, uncomplicated by the country we have become.

There's something about Liverpool's relationship with The Beatles, how for a time the city bristled at them for 'leaving the minute they made a bob' and how they were not sure whether to bury or praise. And that complex set of feelings is requited. Despite The Beatles never really going back, the remaining ones allow themselves to be wheeled out when needed and the dead ones can't prevent it.

The spectacular theme-park version of Liverpool finds the fabs uncomplicated and erects statues to every fart they did — but despite the 'we'll have him' celebrity connection collection that leads Brum to claim everyone from Leeds-based discoverer of Oxygen Joseph Priestley to London and America's thespian David Harewood (and encompassing every glam rocker to come out of the Black Country), Birmingham has made precious little effort to hold on to Hancock.

The city and the man mirror each other, to attempt to sell the connection would be self- parody. The marketeers and promoters of Birmingham can't help themselves, so it has been Hancock himself that stopped us embarrassing everyone again. He did that by simply not giving a fuck, giving a shrug and not looking back over his shoulder. He did the ultimate service to the place that made him; a true Brummie hero. One that wouldn't say he was.

In the famous unguarded and desperately frank *Face to Face* interview on TV he said, "We are all unsure of ourselves, and that is both funny and sad." That should replace our motto on our coat of arms.

JB

What Might Be Under Spaghetti Junction

Billions of people have been on top of Spaghetti Junction, from the early days of the first motorists on 24 May 1972 at about 4.30pm to today. They estimate that around 200,000 cars a day travel on it now, with literally some of these finding the right exit.

But how many have been to experience the wonders beneath?

You could recline on the beach and gaze at the wonderfully complex shapes you get at the meeting point of two motorways, two rivers, three canals, a train line and any number of A- and A(M)-roads. The beach, at Salford Junction, the meeting point of three canals: the Grand Union Canal, Tame Valley Canal and the Birmingham and Fazeley Canal. There's no sand as such, but what is sand but dirt with ideas above its station? And there's plenty of dirt.

Don't think you want to go to Spaghetti on holiday? When it opened, coach operators offered sightseeing tours for 65p each. Their route is a mystery, as is the reason anyone wanted to go on it... except Spaghetti Junction is rather impressive and had been the talk of the local press ever since the design was presented and construction started in 1968.

In the Evening Mail on 1 June 1965 the journalist Roy Smith described plans for the junction as "like a cross between a plate of spaghetti and an unsuccessful attempt at a Staffordshire knot", the headline written by sub-editor Alan Eaglesfield called it 'Spaghetti Junction'. The Mail may have got it wrong as we have a counter-claim on good authority that it was a man from the local authority, Councillor Charles Simpson, who gave it the nickname in a planning meeting. He had heard of an earlier junction in Los Angeles called that (the LA Spaghetti is also apparently known as 'malfunction junction'). We may never know the truth.

It's never clear if Bill Drummond's artworks are the physical objects, the acts of him making them, or something else he decides later. The KLF man, one of the Justified Ancients of Mu Mu, and my favourite artist, is never quite sure what anything means, or can't explain until it's done. This very morning he sent an email in which he informed his fans that he had changed the name of his 'never ending play' from *Never Lock Your Doors* to *Under the Junction*. That junction. "Spaghetti Junction is the entrance to the underworld. Well, according to me it is," he says.

"I kept finding myself returning to the same spot under Spaghetti Junction. I got dropped off at Spaghetti Junction when hitching from Liverpool to my parents' home in Corby. This was in 1973 when I was 19 years old. It was night time and raining. I got lost somewhere deep underneath it all and spent the night there. All very scary."

"In those days hitching was commonplace. My favourite part of the journey was on the elevated stretch of the M6 that cuts through the north and east of Birmingham. [...] From this position the city I could see looked like a city of the future, or at least from the TV programme *Tomorrow's World*. It even had a skyline like American cities had."

I spoke to Bill after seeing the film about his tour *Best Before Death* which opens with him bathing, shrinking his new Levi's, in the canal underneath. I told him that the only other film I knew that featured the underneath of Spaghetti was *Take Me High*, where Cliff zoomed through in a hovercraft. We then spent a good couple of minutes, old men with holes in the mind where Cliff should be, failing to remember the name of the film *Summer Holiday*.

Forgetting can be a good thing; in an episode of *Yes Minister*, civil service chief Sir Humphrey withholds some files as they were "lost in the floods of 1967." "Was 1967 a particularly bad winter?" asks Minister Jim Hacker. "No, a marvellous winter. We lost no end of embarrassing files." The 'floods of 1967' for local gangster lore are large civil engineering projects, particularly the foundations of large road building works, and the largest of road building works in the country was the Gravelly Hill Interchange. So it's no surprise that the 559 concrete columns are rumoured to contain the remains of many enemies of our famous villains. Being around 80% concrete 20% gangster would certainly explain why they continue to need so much repair.

The big rumour is that the concrete is the last resting place of enemies of Eddie Fewtrell, in particular those that fell in The Battle of Snow Hill between the Aston lads and the Kray Twins' army of Cockney villains.

According to sometime Fewtrell doorman Andy, the

"explosion of violence took place on October 14, the date of the Battle of Hastings. Ronnie [Kray] delighted in pointing that out when recalling the carnage. And like Harold's Saxon hordes, the notorious Cockney villains were crushed, their bid to spread the criminal cancer of drugs, extortion and crime to Birmingham streets forever thwarted."

The truth about the battle is very hard to come by, although if someone wants to pay me to make a very long tapestry about it, I'm not an 11th century Norman weaver, but I'll have a look. The best source I can find is a very detailed account in David Keogh's book *The Accidental Gangster*. David is married to Eddie Fewtrell's daughter and claimed to have spoken to many of the Fewtrell clan and others who said they were there, but he then fictionalised it. His book tells of a battle of hundreds, with knives, guns and clubs wrapped in barbed wire, it tells of the Kray gang having their own train to bring the troops from London. If HS2 had been built they may have got here 15 minutes earlier and won, but, eventually, when all seemed lost for the Fewtrells five masked IRA men with machine guns turned up and chased the Krays away. Eddie Fewtrell has since denied any knowledge.

The dead are rumoured to be holding up the M6 (or the A38, or the A5127, rumours are not good traffic reports) but doorman Andy again, "I don't think the construction dates and the battle dates correspond". Who really knows? The construction went on for a long time, there was lots of hardcore needed, and, anyway, these are the foundations of modern Birmingham's myths.

Under Spaghetti Junction is a microcosm of all the things I enjoy about Birmingham: a gritty piece of concrete urbanism that I love but that people assume I appreciate ironically, art that touches on our lives in an ultra-meta way, and a local folk-memory that may or may not have happened. It's where the truth doesn't matter as long as the story is so good.

JB

Sutton Park

OK, we haven't got long. They're watching me now. I'll tell you. But keep it secret. Keep it safe.

Sutton Park is a beautiful, special, place. We will protect it at all costs. I'm going to tell you something of its precious nature and then you can visit, sure, but please don't tell anyone about it.

Sutton Park takes up a sizable chunk of Sutton Coldfield, a Warwickshire town that was reluctantly incorporated into Birmingham in the 1970s and ever since seems to have been trying to leave.

You think you know why Sutton Coldfield is aloof, don't you?

We're a bit up ourselves. Insisting on being called a town, and having our own council running on top of the city council isn't enough for Sutton, oh no. We want to be called *The Royal Town of* Sutton Coldfield too. Many Sutton folks still won't acknowledge that they live in Birmingham, giving their postal address as 'Royal Sutton Coldfield, Warwickshire' (lucky for them, you only really need a postcode and a house number for a letter to actually find a house). At the top end of this game, I've known Sutton people who will address letters to 'Erdington, nr. Birmingham'.

But saying that Sutton has an uneasy alliance with Birmingham is to miss the point that it has an uneasy alliance with everyone else too.

You think this is all down to conservatism (both big and small C) but I think it could be down to its conservationism instead. We're keeping the world at arm's length in case you realise what we have: 2,500 acres of medieval parkland all to ourselves.

The origins of Sutton Park are generally said to be in the establishment of a deer park in the 12th century, but the human history of the land goes back much further. If you walk the park, various orientation markers will give you a sense of the area's ancient history, revealing features such as the Bronze Age burnt mound and the Roman Road to Wall. More modern history also frequently reveals itself to walkers: the rifle butts (off what is formally known as 'Lord Donegal's Ride', more recently the bottom of 'Sandy Hill') reveal some recent martial history, the Jamboree Stone memorialises the worldwide meeting of the Scouting movement on its 50th birthday, and the seven main pools within the park easily give up hints to how they were dammed, tamed and landscaped for fishing, leisure or industry.

For a time, Sutton boasted about the jewel in its royal crown — and it profited too as folk from around the region came up for the day and were charged for the pleasure of it. In an early recorded example of Sutton snootiness, in 1863 it was declared:

"that in order to increase the number and efficiency of the force for maintaining order in the Park and protecting the inhabitants and respectable visitors from the lawless portion of the excursionists the Corporation consider it necessary to impose a payment per head upon all persons entering the Park not being inhabitants (of Sutton Coldfield)"

1879 saw the park directly connected to the rail network, bringing day trippers from ever further afield. A railway advertisement from the 1930s, featuring a beautiful painting of Sutton Park by the commercial artist Michael Reilly, promises visitors "boating, fishing, bathing & golf".

Eventually Beeching's axe would fall on the line through the park (it's still open to freight, and features a terrifying open level-crossing for pedestrians, where the railway line cuts through the Roman road known as Ryknield Street). As far as I can tell, this is when Sutton closed ranks and started keeping the park to itself.

I mean sure, for those who care to look the park is there, but we're not really making much of a case for it and many folk can live in Birmingham for a good stretch without finding it (most of the people I went to uni with had never heard of it, and we spent three years living twenty minutes away from it). By contrast South Birmingham's Cannon Hill Park, which to me is not really a park, just sort of a rubbish big fancy garden with a theatre at one end and swings at the other, seems well known and inexplicably popular.

It's very in keeping with the park's history and future that it could spend 100 years as a tourist attraction, and then spend 100 more trying to fly under the radar. Sutton Park is well protected but it's never preserved — it's not a museum to any one thing but its own essential self, and so the project of its conservation is one of working and changing.

I have a reproduction print of that Michael Reilly railway poster in my kitchen and it's hard to quite place exactly what it shows, but you immediately know it shows Sutton Park. In the painting, an elegant couple are walking toward you next to a sandy track to a lake. The perspective is from the top of a path which leads down to the Bracebridge pool, at a place now known as 'dog beach' because it's a favourite spot for very good boys to have a swim. You can stand on the same spot today but holly has spread toward the path, and birch trees have encroached upon the view. In the future it wouldn't be surprising to find the view opened up once again, as the Sutton Park Ranger team cut back and sculpt the landscape.

The work of the rangers fascinates me — they encourage here, they cut back there. The landscape forever shifts and changes as spaces are opened up by human hands, and then rewild themselves once again. Every year or so whole areas of the park will be totally transformed by conservation work, and this means trees are felled, land is cleared. When I first encountered this it felt destructive and concerning, but I've learned it's part of the rhythm of the park. The Sutton Park I know today won't be the Sutton Park that my grandkids know, nor their children and grandchildren after them, and yet it will always be Sutton Park, in a direct line from the medieval deer park, the place where world scouting met, and Romans marched — the same but different, beautiful and wild, and with a pub on each corner. It's preserved but ever changing. Protected but living. And for now it's my secret, and yours.

JH

Note: Much background reading for this article was done here: sclhrg.org.uk

Our Tradition of Dissent

Dissent has a great tradition in Birmingham.

Although not everyone would agree.

We are the Bartleby the Scrivener of cities, saying "I would prefer not to" to most suggestions and ploughing our own furrow. "Why not build your city around a body of water to give it focus?", "I would prefer not to", "Why not keep your important brutalist buildings?", "I would prefer not to"," "Why not have the actual events in your major sporting festival in the city rather than elsewhere?',"I would prefer not to build a velodrome but we will put some sand down up town for the nudey volleyball."

Who are Birmingham's dissenters? We have a great tradition, the signage people at New Street who refuse to tell you where the platforms are; Caspian Pizza on The Queensway who would not agree that their 'spicy beef' toppings shouldn't be made of lamb; but the most famous dissenter of Birmingham was Joseph Priestley.

Priestley, discoverer of oxygen, inventor of fizzy pop, and resident of Leeds while he was doing that, did cause a big splash in Brum by creating unrest and dragging his Lunar Society crew with him.

Joseph Priestley had attended dinners of 'the Johnson circle' formed around radical bookseller Joseph Johnson, where he would have met such people as Tom Paine, William Blake, or Mary Wollstonecraft and, alongside his founding of British Unitarianism, became a political radical of the most modern kind.

Protestants who rejected the doctrines of the Church of England in the 18th century were referred to as 'dissenters'. Priestley was one of the biggest: a strong believer in complete freedom of worship. He extended this to its logical conclusion, including Roman Catholics and even non-Christians. He was one of the few non-conformist supporters of the Catholic Relief Act of 1791, which introduced formal toleration of Catholic worship and schools. This radicalism was an anathema to many of his fellow dissenters.

John Wesley, the dominant force in Methodism, especially disliked him, declaring Priestley "one of the most dangerous enemies of Christianity". There was even a popular Methodist hymn lampooning Priestley:

> *"Stretch out thy hands, thou Triune God:*
> *The Unitarian fiend expel*
> *And chase his doctrine back to hell."*

Priestley held firm with his views of complete tolerance, and Birmingham was a good place to be for that.

Wesley had visited Birmingham during a tour of the Midlands in 1746 and found people who held views identical to those of the Ranters (a sort of Christian anarchism, notable around the mid 17th century). Wesley, argued against them in horror. "Have you also a right to all the women in the world?" Wesley asked, "Yes, if they consent," was the answer.

Joseph Priestley's radical tolerance annoyed many,

he had attempted to found a reform society, the Warwickshire Constitutional Society, which would have supported universal suffrage and short parliaments and not just a quick walk after dinner. Birmingham was alive with anger over civil rights, the Dissenters' support of the French Revolution, and (apparently) public library book purchases. Their thoughts on ladders go unreported.

The Priestley Riots of July 1791 started with an attack on the Royal Hotel, the site of a banquet organised in sympathy with the French Revolution. The rioters' main target was Joseph Priestley, who had been persuaded not to attend for his own safety. Starting with Priestley's church and home (Fairhill in Sparkbrook), the rioters attacked or burned four dissenting chapels, 27 houses, and several businesses, including the homes of people they associated with Dissenters, such as members of the Lunar Society.

James Watt wrote that the riots "divided [Birmingham] into two parties who hate one another mortally", and presumably Albion fans who everyone tolerates in a patronising manner.

Why did Priestley annoy so many? It may have been that he held a mirror to other people and they did not like that they were not as moderate as they felt they were. "He made them look into their own souls and realise there was nothing there, and that made them crazy." said the comedian Alexei Sayle, who was talking about why many people got so angry with Jeremy Corbyn.

The English radical tradition which stretches back to the Ranters and the Diggers through Priestley and the

Dissenters to people like Jeremy Corbyn is not well served by our history-teaching, which is Elizabeth I and the Second World War, with a diversion towards the hats of the fictional Peaky Blinders if you're in Birmingham. If we are to break it down, it can be as simple as refusal to let harm to others continue, to stand up in a moral way: and Birmingham, with its innate pig-headedness, is a place where the tradition can be seen.

One of the radicals that makes me most proud at the moment is the MP for Coventry South, Zarah Sultana. Despite being MP for Coventry, Zarah was raised in Lozells, and exhibits a properly Brummie sense of self: "Why not, once you've become an MP, play along with Murdoch, get a makeover for the Sunday Times magazine and play with corporate interests?", "I would prefer not to, bab," she says.

Clare Short was the most high profile MP in Birmingham until she left parliament in 2010, and her time in office was characterised by taking on powerful interests, including the misogyny of Rupert Murdoch's media. Her radical influence would have been felt by a young Sultana, if she had any interest in politics. Her mum and dad were members of the Labour Party — but, she says, "that didn't really mean anything". Well, it was the Blair era.

She tells a story to demonstrate what made her a radical: a senior police officer from the West Midlands Police force (Chief Supt. Tom Coughlan) claimed during a meeting of the city council's equalities scrutiny committee he could walk into Holte School in Wheeler

Street, and "every child would be able to name the gang that they saw themselves joining in the future".

That, and the installation of 'terror camera' CCTV to spy on residents around Sparkbrook made her realise how those in positions of power viewed her community: "Because of our postcode, because of our skin colour, because of our class." Eventually the residents got the cameras removed, they stood their moral ground.

In Zarah's maiden speech she called out "40 years of Thatcherism", and sent the media into spirals of rebuttal, but she has on this and many other issues stood firm. If we are to move the country on from those 40 years, if we are to get anywhere, we will need more people like Zarah Sultana, more who won't be distracted from what is right. It makes me proud that Birmingham still produces people like this, people in the best tradition of dissent, who will say 'no' when it is needed. Why not just admit Birmingham is shit? I would prefer not to.

JB

That Distinctively Nothing Skyline

As is often the case, we can blame the TV show *Frasier*.

It's the early 2000s, and I pay my bills doing website and graphic design. We're presenting initial concepts for a branding project, and the client says these words — words that, in a very short career, I've come to dread:

"For the logo, could we try a Birmingham skyline?"

We hem and we haw, we hear them (we say) and we try to lead them another way.

"I really do think the Birmingham skyline would make it pop."

We ask if instead they'd like us to tr—

"No I really do want to see it with a Birmingham skyline."

And so a week later, we meet up, and show some more work. And it just doesn't. It doesn't pop. Not a bit.

"Oh I thought it would be more distinctive than that."

Well, it really isn't: local heart, global city (nondescript).

If you think about that *Frasier* logo, the one with the skyline, what really makes it pop is the Space Needle — a distinctive building that places you instantly in Seattle.

For Paris you'd have the Eiffel Tower, New York has the Statue of Liberty and Empire State, while Newcastle and Bristol are blessed with distinctive bridges.

It's not that Birmingham doesn't have distinguished buildings and structures. People have come to the second city and done architecture upon it. We have the much-demolished brutalist buildings of John Madin, the faux-classical grandeur of Victoria Square (the Council House, Town Hall and galleries), and larger civil engineering works such as the Gravelly Hill Interchange at Spaghetti Junction. Yet somehow when put together, this all fails to become a skyline.

Birmingham will defy anyone who wants to distil its urban environment into a line drawn cityscape. What is its Space Needle? Try to outline the Rotunda as a 2D line drawing and instead of a distinctive cylinder you have just a modestly tall rectangle. Try to draw her skyline and Birmingham will simply give you a low sprawl of warehouses and shopping malls with the sideways arse of Selfridges on the end.

Let's be honest, they never stood a chance.

It's 2008, and Birmingham City Council are once again the butt of the joke. The joke is different most weeks, but this week the joke is: they don't even know what their own skyline looks like.

In celebration of the city's great success at recycling, the council printed and distributed 72,000 leaflets. And on these leaflets, a hero image that showed the skyline of Birmingham. Birmingham, Alabama. USA.

It is unknown how successfully they were recycled but the leaflets did bring the city's lack of skyline into the wider consciousness as that week's 'you couldn't make it up' news story. I don't blame anyone at the council for not being able to tell they'd spent £15,000 on leaflets with the wrong city skyline on them because how could they possibly tell? They decided to run with a picture of absolutely nothing meaningful to anyone at all. They chose to use an image of a big smudge of nothing, very similar to our own big smudge of nothing in a lot of ways.

We can only assume that somebody, somewhere, thought it would pop.

I can see my house from up here

It's late October 2020, in the dying days of the first flush of the COVID-19 pandemic. I'm running out from Four Oaks, cutting through the fancy golf course at Little Aston, skimming the edge of Aldridge and looping back toward Streetly.

I've been out in the suburbs now since March. On most days I walk or I run, using up my allotted time outdoors, my state sanctioned one trip a day for exercise and wellbeing.

Erdington Road is a long stretch between fields that runs roughly parallel to the Chester Road. On my right (the western side) there's a steep climb, on the other side it's a much flatter run off toward Sutton Park via Streetly Crematorium and the Veseyans rugby ground. Soon I'll hit the junction with Foley Road (which has both types of Brummie waypoints — a pub *and* an island), and I'll cut right and start to make that climb.

It's been strange to be cut off from the city. I work from home, so I only go into town to do things — gigs, movies, birthday parties, drinks with friends and meals out. I probably would often go whole months without a trip to Brum-proper without a second thought, but being told 'no' is very different to not being arsed with it. When you're cut off from it all, you start to feel a little loss you never knew you'd feel.

As the hill starts to top out, I can pull off the pavement on a trail. There's something of a ridgeline here over common land and past trees, toward a bandstand-like structure: the Barr Beacon War Memorial.

The actual trig point at Barr Beacon is fenced inside the adjacent water works, so the memorial is the public high point. They say you can see 11 English and Welsh counties from the Beacon, with views of the Lickey Hills, Cannock Chase and The Wrekin on offer. But what I'm really here for today is Birmingham.

There she is.

There's a touch of morning mist about and the light is slow and fat as it rolls across the vista in front of me.

I push on back toward the road which will drop down toward Great Barr and The Asda at Queslett. Brum lies before me, a flat sprawl, a carpet of glowing red house bricks that eventually yields to the outer industrial core of Newtown and then on to the Gun Quarter.

Somewhere in the Pheasey Estate someone has set up a back garden PA and, with no deference to the early hour, they're belting out some tuneful but unknowable Irish folk songs to play me back into my city.

The BT Tower is a distinctive shape from here but Old Joe in Selly Oak eludes me for the moment. I start to reconnect with all the other parts of the city I've missed. Down there is the River Tame and its namesake canal cousin. The train from Perry Barr out to Walsall runs across this tableau. Over to my left Villa Park is waiting to be filled again. I can't see these things from here but I know them, and can feel them. If this view has no shape then how can it be so full of associations?

I never really stop on a run, but today I do; I stop for a second to drink in that nothing skyline. And just there on that hill, for once, it finally pops.

JH

The Jasper Carrott LP in Your Dad's Record Collection

Our front room contained a host of treasures, not just the colour TV and a settee that seemed like sitting on a cloud. It also was where Dad's record collection was.

My dad's record collection was LPs of a certain type of singer, Brill Building songwriters like James Taylor, the fey folk of Melanie and the room-clearing (of my mum anyway) poetry of Leonard Cohen. Later, we got an integrated stereo and alongside the vinyl there appeared a few tapes. Not bought ones, but orange-stickered and hand-written copies.

The main cassette I remember was one labelled 'Jeff Wayne's News of the World' copied for him by his mate Big Al. I don't recall what was on it, but the chances of anything coming from Wayne's Ma's to borrow his copy and read Hagar the Horrible were slim.

It's fair to say that the contents of my dad's record collection were not that interesting to me as a small boy. Songs of love and hate, and friendly and amicable divorces in the California sunshine didn't hit the spot with those of us raised on Adam Ant videos on Saturday morning TV. But there was one LP I liked. Yellow, and looking a bit like the end of Bugs Bunny cartoons with the thick circles. There was a man dressed as a rabbit on the back too.

I didn't get to listen to it.

I am listening to it as I type, the record part of my inheritance. The content part of my culture.

A hiss when he mentions he lives in Solihull, a routine about the opening of Spaghetti Junction that rests heavily on the fact that bolognese sounds a bit like bollocks in a Brummie accent. All hot on the grooves of an in-joke of the audience being taught how to clap, this is the comedian doing all the local gags, but not to get the audience on side, rather to cement that this is a club in the joining sense and he's the entertainment secretary.

The routines are as familiar to me as the feel and pattern of bus-seat material. It contains the one about being a blues fan in the wrong end at Man United, the one where a reporter says "he's fucked off, Tone" live on BRMB to Tony Butler, and *The Magic Roundabout*.

The *The Magic Roundabout* routine goes down so rapturously it's obvious the crowd is already in on the joke. This is a greatest hits set. It's like Carrott arrived fully formed, he mentions that he has just done his first national radio broadcast, but apart from the 'dickhead' sign and the insurance forms routines, this album, this live performance, contains the essence of Jasper. He's brought his guitar but he doesn't play it.

It doesn't contain *Funky Moped*, and it isn't especially funny, but it doesn't matter. Dads love Jasper, and those from Birmingham particularly like to share the clip from his series *The Detectives*, where he's heard singing 'Shit on the Villa' over a wire-tap. Jasper, as a famous Brummie, and one of the first stand-up comedians to emerge from the folk clubs, gets more than a pass, he gets unconditional status as one of all of our extended families.

The best bit about the LP? The legend 'Recorded Live in Erdington'.

You can smell the Ansells Mild, and the record sounds like home.

JB

The German Market, Yes, The German Market (Hear Me Out)

I'm not going to argue that the German Market isn't shit. Its shiteness is self-evident and widely talked about. It's easy to slag it off, so first I will. There are crowds of people with no idea how to act or move in crowds. There's the eye-damage from stray umbrella spokes. And there's overpriced tat and foul tasting sweets sold from the same five or six stalls repeated over and over again. Over and over again like a twisted parody of the shops in your pisshole suburb's high street. The high street that you've just come from on a bus that manages to be both clammy with condensation and uncomfortably full of coat. To drink, there's headache beer and migraine wine liberally over-served to once-a-year drinkers. The weather is almost consistently a mixture of sleet and hail, so perfectly calibrated for its bleakness it's enough to make you believe in an intelligent creator; and that he hates us.

For the longest time, people loved the German Market. To all Brummies it's 'The German Market' no matter how hard the PR hacks push its real name, or how large they print the words on the banner. People would meet after work, parents would bring their kids, and hating it became akin to labeling yourself Scrooge McBastard and filming yourself buggering an elf on a shelf. But hate it I did. It's unfair to label me a contrarian because that would imply some reactionary element, I'm not a contrarian, I'm just a weirdo.

But the German Market lost its shine. The prices, that were always a little high, carried on inflating while peoples' wages were stretched a little further. Its popularity grew but the infrastructure to support it lagged. The local shops came to resent the two full months of having a carnival full of office drunks on their doorstep, and there's only so many wooden croaking frogs you can buy your other half for Christmas before they start pissing in your morning coffee.

For a brief and glorious minute the public consensus and I were simpicato. I wasn't expecting sky writing or a big party with 'you were right all along' banners, but a card might have been nice. Bastards. This, however, was to be short-lived. My editor (one of the other writers of this book, Jon Bounds) challenged me to write something in defence of the German Market. So I spent a very cold day from when it opened to near enough when it closed and wrote a nuanced and thoughtful piece called 'Hate The German Market, Buy a Candle and Shut the Fuck Up'.

The thing I realised is that indeed, the Frankfurt Christmas Market is shit, but everything about Christmas is a little shit. The films, the songs, the parties, the food, all of it is fifty shades of shite. But that's not the point: we not only endure them, we love them. Not despite the hokey saccharine artifice but because of it. The magic of Christmas is a suspension of our cynical adult brains, we drop the cool, the cynical, and jaded and wrap ourselves in the rituals and traditions we all share. We eat dry turkey, suffer the same cracker jokes and hide the same Lynx gift sets until we can re-gift them next year: because the things are rarely the thing. The love is the thing, the love is the point.

And if we decide that the way to show my friends I love them is standing in god's own punishing sleet, drinking overpriced beer that will definitely give me a headache, I will gladly do it and keep the glass as a souvenir. Not because I need a heavy pint glass, as I said, the thing isn't the thing. The pint glass is a night shared laughing with my friends.

Birmingham isn't shit, but Christmas is, and that's why we love it.

DS

Boon (Series 1-3 only)

Plans to erect a colossus-like statue of Michael Elphick over Broad Street have never got off the imaginary drawing board in my head. Despite that, I still think it would be a massive *Boon* for the area.

Boon is a story of friendship and courage, and motorbikes. Ken Boon (Elphick in rugged form) is a medically retired firefighter who ends up doing 'Anything Legal' after an ex-colleague (David Daker as Harry, now running a hotel) puts an ad in the paper looking for interesting work for him. From series two Neil Morrissey's long haired and stereotypically dense Brummie Rocky joins them and they have adventures.

It's difficult to explain how big *Boon* was, top of the ratings for ITV, seven series and a feature length Christmas special. It spawned a top five hit record — Jim Diamond's *Hi Ho Silver (The Theme from Boon)* — and a film *I Bought a Vampire Motorcycle* which was shot, so the rumour says, in between series to give the cast and crew something to do. Running 'on blood, not petrol', it's a campy, pulpy, horror, but set in the back streets of Brum. In particular it's set under the same railway arch on Floodgate Street, again and again. As the gravelly trailer voice-over says "the vampire motorcycle could be right up your street".

My favourite bit of the first episode of *Boon* is when they couldn't afford to do a second take of the shot of Ken's fire engine coming out of the station and so had to use the one where a WMPTE bus cut across the frame. *Boon* could have been set anywhere, but when they need a newspaper they use the Birmingham Evening Mail, when they need to go to the newspaper office they go to the Post and Mail Building, John Madin and Partners' own Brummie colossus.

Boon had deep roots in Brum, but before series four Central TV moved most of its operations from Broad Street to Nottingham, and took Ken, Harry and the bikes with it.

The Birmingham of *Boon* (series 1-3 only) is preserved as it was, not the side glances of buildings presented as if they were nowhere, as if they were anywhere else, nor a knowing historical narrative. Not *Spooks*'s fictional London, not *Line of Duty*'s fictional everytown, not *Crossroads*'s fictional wobbly village, not the fictional working class of *Peaky Blinders* or *Benefit Street*. It is real, for no other reason than the producers made it so. Even the pets were real Brummie pets: my mate's dog had a bit part.

Boon (series 1-3 only) stands as a monument to a Birmingham that has since been dug up, knocked down, sandblasted, polished and clad, and is about to be knocked down again. The constant re-invention, born I'm sure of the insecurity of the middle child, means our history is seen only in flashes. It can be completely hidden, it doesn't even get repeats up the top of the EPG.

My primary school divided us into houses — not with a magical hat or to any great end, there weren't enough kids for us to play against each other at anything — and they were named after the famous industrialists buried in the church over the road. I was in Watt, the others in Boulton and Murdoch, but I'm not sure the houses did anything but provide a little competition sometimes to let off steam: the history of the men wasn't a topic we covered. Despite it being in Handsworth and a good amount of black history being touched upon, there was no connecting of those men and slavery.

Birmingham's most famous statue, called 'The Carpet Salesmen' by local journalists and not at all by others, is a gold-plated representation of Watt, Boulton and Murdoch looking at some plans. It was sculpted by William Boye and unveiled in 1956, standing outside the then Register Office on Broad Street. The book *Solid Citizens — Statues in Birmingham* by Bridget Pugh from the early 80s considers it the centrepiece of our tributes to the Lunar Society.

There is not a lot of history in the book, more a list of 'great men' cast in stone (plus Queen Victoria and 'the smallest woman'), but the past is not cast in stone, it's open to our investigation and interpretation. We may congratulate ourselves that Brum has avoided having too many prominent statues of those associated with slavery; expect that we've achieved that by putting pretty much all the of the prominent statues in storage or out of the way.

Dr Nathaniel Adam Tobias ~~Coleman~~[1], born and based in Birmingham, is an academic and activist who is writing a book about our collective memory of the colonial and anti-colonial arguments by which Birmingham built and attempted to abolish the British Empire. He talks about the narrative about statues and slavery and how it's not adequate to add context, and how it's black people in particular who should take control of the debate: even in terms of which statues are talked about.

We could make a case that the Industrial Revolution ran on blood as well as steam, we could put all these statues in plain sight and add plaques but as Dr ~~Coleman~~ says, "why block views with marble"?

But if we are to change the statue story, why not remove the dead men, unblock the views and celebrate Ken Boon? I think there is real precedent to celebrate Boon's capture of, and impact on the city. If we are to have statues, and real people are always going to be problematic, then fictional characters can represent us. There's a statue of Paddington Bear in Paddington station, the Little Mermaid in Copenhagen, Peter Faulk as Columbo in Budapest for no reason anyone can fathom and, one more thing, there's even one of Stallone as Rocky in Philadelphia.

Do we leave the Watt statue in a warehouse in Nechells until the redevelopment finishes and restore it with a 'context giving' plaque? He should stay there. As we know, Birmingham will never be finished.

Not until there's a statue of Ken Boon.

JB

1   Nathaniel Adam Tobias ~~Coleman~~ is the son of a Jamaican immigrant who grew up in Birmingham with his single mother, Lorrel, and his three siblings. He strikes through his last name as his family was given it when they were purchased from Jamaica.

The Northfield Sunset, or The Corner of Lockward Road and the Sir Herbert Austin Way Bypass During the Months of June, July, and August at Around Seven O'Clock

No matter how hard you try there are always some things about yourself you can't change, you can lie, obfuscate, and fight against but they will remain immutable truths. I will always have been born in the 70s, my eyes will always be on the grey side of blue, and no matter where I go, what I do, or how I act I will always be from Northfield.

I grew up to the sound of police helicopters at night circling the housing estate on Ley Hill, car alarms, or listening to the local gang's two tone whistle they used as some sort of aural territory marker or to call for help from streets away. My childhood wasn't a bad one, but to deny that the piss-stained concrete and carrier bags flapping on barbed wire aesthetic didn't affect me in some fundamental way would be a lie.

I wasn't a typical Northfield boy. Rather than learning to ride a bike, or playing kerbie, I spent my pre-teen years reading my way through Northfield library to the point where I ran out of kids' books to read. To their credit, they then let me start reading the adult books, which I also read through. Even the Eric Van Lustbader novel that had more sex than the actual ninjas that I'd picked it up for in the first place. I did do normal Northfield things though, I got banned from Grosvenor Shopping Centre for life three or four times. The pinnacle of these was in my twenties when after an afternoon skating in the car park on the roof, we got locked in. This left me walking around the closed mall trying not to freak out in that liminal space. Luckily, being a good Northfield boy, I noticed that one of the doors wasn't locked in any serious way and we were able to escape. I was never formally banned for that one, but I avoided the place nonetheless for months.

Northfield hasn't changed much, and my love/hate relationship with it hasn't either. To walk through Northfield in 2021 is to walk through it in the 1980s: the same litter, the same mothers smoking over open pushchairs, the same gnarled old bastards on the way to or from the fruit machines, the same 15 variations of the same shop, dog shit, desperation, and decay. When they talk about 'levelling up', places like Northfield are forgotten.

It would be simpler to just hate it but it's also woven into my DNA so I have to find peace with it somehow. There are some absolute heroes that spend their lives making Northfield a better place. It's an honour to share a postcode with Olly Armstrong, a local politician but all-round good human, and the B31 Voices blog guys care in a way my black little heart stopped being able to years ago.

There is joy in Northfield: the foxes at five in the morning roaming the streets like they have a license to, Victoria Park is the very definition of a hidden gem and Hill Top Park has one of the best hills for sledding in Birmingham. And — and this is the best thing — during the summer months you can turn off the main high street and just before you get to the bypass look down Lockward Road as it drops down the hill to an unobstructed view of the sky, going from the enveloping bleak gray of small-town Birmingham to being faced with the majesty of a summer sunset over the hills in the distance. You have to catch your breath at a sky smeared with reds and pinks, it reminds you that even though you're an urban animal, the woods are never that far away.

DS

The Lilac Time

In the early-viral period (post-fax machine, post-email chain of 'Tommy Cooper jokes', but pre-TikTok sea shanties on the six-o'clock news) there was a 'you know you're a Brummie when' list going around and one of the answers hit the spot. It was 'you don't think there's anything odd in your three favourite bands being ELO, UB40 and Black Sabbath', and I think the point is that the people of Birmingham prize local feeling above more traditionally liking similar kinds of music: an eclectic taste enabled by a dogmatic desire not to travel.

I'm guilty of this too, although for UB40 (any of them) replace Dexy's, and for Black Sabbath (who I appreciate, but can't listen to) replace The Lilac Time.

Really this is about the words and music of Stephen Duffy. They all have shards of Birmingham that run through them. Not big songs about the city, but songs that take place where they do because they — in his experience, our experience — couldn't have happened anywhere else.

Holte End Hotel (from *Music in Colours* with Nigel Kennedy from 1993) is his most direct song about a place — "I'll meet you where the lane from Witton stalls," it says, with reference to Andy Lochhead and the then-derelict pub's "ballroom days". Many of us have our memories take place in pubs that are no longer there, many of our memories are burnt down and recuperated, and some of us look askance at Doug Ellis when it happens.

I asked Stephen about his habit of slipping Brum

in. "We share a mythology. But the places we shared, sometimes whole roads have gone. Barbarellas. The art college in Fazeley Street, The Golden Eagle" he says, "looking back now I still feel as if I'm only 17 and every record feels like it's my first one I've ever made, and the Birmingham that I grew up in feels like a completely different place altogether. Living only in my dreams"

"When the fabric of the place where you spent your childhood changes so dramatically you end up with a bigger story. I was born in Highfield Road in Alum Rock. Someone came and delivered a sofa to me, they were from Birmingham and when I said I was from Highfield Road they thought I was joking. The factories are all fields now! All the pubs have been knocked down… the Pelham Arms, no the Ward End, is still there."

"When I lived in Los Angeles I bumped into Jeff Lynne and within minutes we were talking about the Rock Cinema. It turns out we both went to the same careers office in Burney Lane. I don't think they told either of us to write pop songs, but I asked him why he left Brum and he said 'the lock ins'."

Brummies navigate by pubs, even our memories. I think architects James & Lister Lea had a lot to do with that, they have a style that helps guide you, tall terracotta frontages, tipsy trig points to our past. Inside, if they are still there, the tiles froth with history, even if the beer is flat and there are no pubs like this anywhere else… Step into The Woodman or The Barton Arms and you can only be in a James & Lister Lea pub, listen to The Lilac Time and you can only be in our shared imagined past.

Facebook has killed collective nostalgia, or at least mortally wounded it with a sharpened racist Minion meme, made the past not rose- or sepia-tinted but angrily white. Through song, through the memory of a poet, a fleeting glimpse caught in an advertising mirror behind the optics, you can just about take it. Stephen Duffy does it best, because he's a Brummie:

"I don't know whether people from Birmingham are more immediately nostalgic than anyone else, but you leave school and there's someone trying to arrange a reunion already. Perhaps people from Birmingham do have a slightly more sentimental nature to them and I think that's probably — in our case — something to do with the Irish/Scottish maudlin Celtic strain in our family."

The Lilac Time are named from a line in Nick Drake's *River Man*, "Going to see the river man / Going to tell him all I can / About the plan / For lilac time". What the writer meant, I'm not sure — a plan to watch the 1928 Gary Cooper film perhaps — but the haze of Nick Drake's music is a warm fuzzy nostalgia, the yeasty fug of the second pint of Brew XI on a winter's afternoon. Drake was from Tanworth-in-Arden, the filming location for the village of King's Oak in *Crossroads*, a location chosen to feel like an imagined past already in the early 60s.

Unlike ELO, who are in every dad's car, or Dexy's or UB40, who are at every wedding reception, it's not easy to find The Lilac Time. You might hear *Kiss Me* at a disco, but it used to be the case that you read about most music long before you heard it. If the artist was interesting enough and the writer good enough then you would file their name in your head or perhaps a notebook — for when you had money and chanced upon a second hand copy.

A loving article about folk music and ecstasy in Dazed and Confused and a vinyl copy of *& Love for All* (The Lilac Time's third LP, from 1990) picked up in a basement fire-sale on the Tottenham Court Road in 1990 was my journey to the world of Stephen Duffy. A world that has been rewarding and mysterious: a half-heard rumour of a new record, a film that never quite makes it, a lyric (from the song *Twenty Three*) that asks "I sang my songs of Birmingham, how did you relate to them?"

"When I lived in Los Angeles I bumped into Jeff Lynne and within minutes we were talking about the Rock Cinema. It turns out we both went to the same careers office in Burney Lane. I don't think they told either of us to write pop songs but I asked him why he left Birmingham and he said 'the lock ins'."

The sheer joy of shared experience elevates the songs, but Birmingham does produce poetry as well as noise. Pubs produce poetry, a retelling of our daily lives into anecdote and a transformation of hardship and loss into laughter. Like pub tales, these songs encompass the ideal versions of our lives and get better in the telling. Like pubs, like the city we remember together, they get knocked down.

"Yes, we have always been guilty of self-mythologising," says Stephen Duffy, "You have to write it down. I have to sing about Birmingham because I worry we might look back and nothing's there." ***JB***

A Small Enough City That You Can Learn It

London is rubbish, isn't it? You know that in your bones, you feel it in your soul. But why? What do you hate so much about the idea of London?

No, it's not all the Cockneys (they're not even really real, are they? Just various shades of doing the voice). No it's not 'Westminster elites'. They're crap, true, but it turns out that most of them are from all over the country (that's the way the representative part of representative democracy works). And it's not the super rich, because they don't really have a bearing on anyone's day-to-day life (they're not being slow on the self-service checkout, putting their bins out early, or having a house party — in fact they're rarely even there and when they are they exist in a parallel dimension of weird rich stuff).

Birmingham is not shit, but London is. And here's why.

London is vast, unknowable and hard work. Birmingham on the other hand is compact, understandable and easy to learn. Brum is big enough to be exciting and to offer you prospects but small enough that you can actually grasp what its deal is quickly and then lean into it a bit, have some fun with it, and play in the space.

There's a small group of my school friends who ended up drifting into London for work, and they see me more often than they see each other because London manages to get in the way of living well (they're most likely to see each other if they happen to go home to their parents at the same time). The only time it's hard to see a mate who lives at the other end of town in Birmingham is if they close the tunnels for a repaint.

When I first came to Birmingham it felt like everywhere was a five quid taxi ride away, and it was easy to learn the basic layout of the city (even if it seems to be made up of a thousand quarters). Before too long I knew the differences between Balsalls Common and Heath, where each of the city's Worlds End Roads led, and that you'd always find defaced street signs on Dogpool Lane, Rea St, and Farthing Lane. Once you learn about spaces and places, you quickly learn history and in-jokes too: from the back of Rackhams to taking people up the Ackers, Birmingham joyously gives up its memes and cultural memory to newcomers and asks them to join in the fun. Birmingham is so easy to grasp, in fact, that if you aren't careful you end up writing the book on it.

JH

The Austin Social Club

It's said that home is a place that "when you have to go there, they have to take you in", but can it be a place where you've never really felt that at-home?

My family have been going to the Austin Social Club, or just 'The Austin', for as long as I can remember. I have generations of memories of that place which I can only place into any real timeline by gauging how tall I am comparatively against my dad's legs or the varying shitness of the haircuts. Nearly every occasion that would warrant it would have one of the function rooms booked with a DJ and a nice spread done by one of the family, usually my nan. Some still drink there and my brother and both my parents are members.

But I was never quite comfortable — I was a queer kid (in every sense of that word). Not being interested in football excluded me from every male conversation, my clothes are a subculture soup rather than 'name' brands, vintage re-issue sportswear and polo shirts. And the parties I mentioned? I usually spent them under a table reading. That or sitting with my mom trying not to notice the diagonal looks in my direction, waiting for the big drama and inevitable fight that would signal the end of the night. No small amount of times involving my brother, Craig.

Tonight I've asked my brother to sign me in. "Look after him," my mother warns, I point out that he's a grown ass man himself pushing 40, and built like Harambe, "You know what I mean," she says. And I do, although part of the reason I asked him is for him to look out for me.

"How do I look?" I ask Lucy, my girlfriend. I'm wearing plain black jeans and a plain black T-shirt. I can't do anything about my heavy black boots because they're the only shoes I have. And I really can't do anything about my neon yellow hair.

"Why do you care? You don't usually."

"Dunno."

Craig is already inside when I get there, I text him so he can sign us in. The Austin Sports and Social Club is two flat buildings either side of a small road behind a car park, a train station, and one of those electrical substations that look like a Jack Kirby depiction of a future planet. Until recently you could step out of the large entrance gates and if you looked up the road, be able to see the window of the flat I spent much of my first four years on this planet.

The buildings on the left contain the Metro and the President Suite function rooms, which are named after models of the car produced by the Rover plant that dominated the area up until nearly ten years ago. Before the rebranding the club was called the 'Austin Apprentices' Club' named after the training buildings for the factories that were here before. The building on the right is the club-proper made up of a bar, lounge, and the 'concert room'.

The entrance is wood and looks the way entrances to

social clubs have looked since anyone can remember. My brother opens the door. The entrance doors and exit are separated by a panel and an old woman in the ticket booth carefully signs us in. Through the sliding window I can see her wordsearch book and small television on her desk.

On a large display of photos in the hallway there are people wearing shirts and the maroon Rover Group club tie. We pass an alcove with some fruit machines, which have dividers which I presume are to shield the inviting blinking from young eyes, although whatever temptation they potentially offer is offset by the expression of the guy still in his work clothes joylessly feeding money in with resigned and defeated concentration.

The concert room is being used, the slap and hum of a rock and roll double bass carrying down the hall. Even if you were only a teenager in the 50s you'd be nearly 80 by now. But then again I still listen to music from 50 years ago so maybe it's not that odd.

The lounge is decorated in pastel browns and soft yellows, inoffensive, like a room for grieving relatives in a village hospital.

On the right there's a DJ kit dominating the raised area which one group is still squeezing past to sit in, what I assume are, their regular seats. Opposite are a group of dour looking people, explained by the giant banner with an older man's face and 'RIP' in massive letters.

"I think he used to work here," says Craig.

The bar is obscured by the fence that corrals people

into a queuing system. The pool table at the back is dominated by kids playing their own version of pool which seems to involve a lot fewer cues than I normally play with. Next to it is a hatch where the food is served.

"The food is pretty good here actually," Craig seems as surprised as anyone else at this, as a styrofoam box is passed to someone.

"I'll be alright I reckon."

The door behind the pool table leads to a kids' play area where a bulk of the children seem to be.

I see where we're heading. My uncle John is sitting in the middle with his brother's kids (my cousins? I can never keep it straight in my head, big families do that), their kids and their friends around two tables. A massive flat screen TV is next to the table playing snooker but no-one seems to be paying attention to it. Opposite our tables are a family of what I presume to be brothers, all of similar ages and strikingly the same features. None of them seem to be talking or smiling which adds to the uncanny effect. My uncle on the other hand is sitting and smiling serenely. Years ago his nickname was 'Ginger John' but now just seems to be John as various people approach him throughout the night to buy him a drink and shake his hand. I can tell when we sit down my brother has been keeping pace with my uncle. Which is a mistake. My uncle can *drink* drink. He's a man that used to use Archers as a mixer with his brandy. I mean my brother is no slouch himself, but him keeping up with Uncle John is exactly what my mom was warning me about when she said for me to look after him. My uncle asks what we're having.

"I'll get my own UJ, we can't get into rounds with you," I say, Uncle John looks confused.

"That's not what I asked. I said 'what you having?'" he leans into it a little.

"Pint of Carling dash and Lucy will have a Strongbow."

Craig has told everyone why I'm here.

"So what's this book you're writing?" I explain roughly what the project is.

"So what you got so far?" someone asks, my brain freezes

"Eeeerrr… scallops?" I say

"OooooOOOOOoooo," says the table, "can't beat a good scallop on the way home," they agree. They begin pitching their own suggestions.

"How about the McDonald's ramp?" says one of my cousin's friends.

"Yes, I've already done that one. I wrote about it being the centre of town." I leave out the Joseph Conrad framing, not that I don't think they'll get it: I just don't want to feel like a snob or a swot. Why does this place make me feel like this? I excuse myself to the toilet.

The music from the concert room is a Slade cover, jumping ahead to the 70s. There's a little vending box next to the toilet that sells lottery cards where you rip off a panel to see if you've won. Inside the gents' one of the urinals has four or five of them dropped in, they've been pissed on.

Back in the lounge everybody has turned and is facing my empty chair. The football is on. Apparently Birmingham City are playing West Brom. Now, even though it is technically a local derby, the Austin is a majority of Blues fans and there aren't any Baggies in here, but there are enough Villa fans by default supporting West Brom to keep it spicy. The game, I have to say, is one of the worst I've seen: neither team covering themselves in glory but Albion getting the points.

As soon as the final whistle is blown the DJ begins playing the John Williams *Superman* theme. Through the usual DJ mouth too close to the microphone mumble I manage to catch his name is Dave. This makes sense as for this pantheon of family friends the naming convention seems to be alliteration, Bill the Butcher is a good friend of Uncle John, Ginger John, despite my nan sometimes seeing Mick the Meat for her Sunday roast.

A woman from the grieving party is invited up, wobbly voiced she thanks some people. Most everyone in the room is struggling to make out what she's saying, at one point her voice breaks and has to stop to stifle sobs. The whole room breaks out in supportive applause. When she toasts at the end everybody raises their glass.

On another trip to the loo the concert room has the unmistakable sound of 80s synth.

My uncle is drinking at what for me is a reckless pace

and I'm somehow caught in the round with him. He tells me I'm 'in the chair', so I go to the bar and order the round. I forget to say please, which I hastily add at the end.

"That's alright love," says the girl behind the bar "we know what you mean". One of the older ladies by the crisps and nuts tells me: "We like your hair".

"Glad you noticed," I say, setting her up.

"Well you can't exactly miss it!" there it is, we laugh.

I ask my uncle about drinking here. In my memory this was always his second choice. He was a regular at the King George V up the road. Even after it had been turned into an Indian restaurant him and his friends would crowd the tiny bar.

"Well, I always came here for dos and things."

"But why here now, is it just that it's close?" I ask. My cousin Emma interjects "Well put it like this, someone just came over and handed in the Nintendo DS that had been left on the table over there. In fact they've all got phones and things and they all get handed in. Can you imagine that happening anywhere else?"

Another person interrupts to shake Uncle John's hands and offer him a drink. It's starting to feel like a mob wedding, my uncle a capo everyone pays respect to as they pass.

"Percentage wise, how many of the people in this room do you know by name?"

"About 50, the rest I've probably forgotten".

Lucy has been impressive in keeping up the pace and comes back from the bar with another round and a selection of scratchings and crisps. "Brummie tapas," shouts someone over the music and the bags are split down the side and opened in the middle of the table.

In no time my uncle has finished his pint and gestures to mine. "Alright, but it's the last one, I've got to get everyone back," I'm not driving but Uncle John knows what I mean. He laughs as he gets up: "You always was weird, but I love ya."

As we leave I can hear the club singer rendition of a Simply Red song, it seems a shame to leave because at this pace in three hours' time they will be singing songs from a decade in the future. But we say our goodbyes and leave.

Who I am is made from a bunch of things in and out of my control. And as I've got older I've realised as much as I've had to negotiate my relationship with my family, my family have had to come to terms with me, an anomaly. Something they have done with a lot more grace and less conflicted resentment than I managed. Despite this we've settled into a state of bemused acceptance. One thing I do know though, with absolute certainty, is that they will always, always, be there for me. Whether I want them or not, when I need them they'll be there for me.

And if I do need them, I know exactly where they'll be.

DS

Mr Blue Sky

Birmingham, as the Jane Austen quote misused by broadsheet feature writers says, has "something direful in the sound": we are painted as dull, as boring. And particularly by a media based in London who definitely can't see the point of any train that comes here at all, let alone one that does it 20 minutes faster.

Even ELO genius Jeff Lynne is described on Wikipedia as "a native of Birmingham [with] a flat Brummie accent" (from a Daily Telegraph review).

How odd then, that his song, the song that most defines the city, was voted the 'happiest song ever' in one of those polls that companies commission for publicity. It ran away down the avenue with a fifth of the vote. How odd then, that everyone loves the record but shows disdain for the town that made it. How odd then, that Jeff is responsible for some of the brightest and most euphoric music ever to come from anywhere. He also worked on some Ringo Starr solo material; which at least can make you laugh.

Mr Blue Sky has been chosen on Desert Island Discs many times, including by cyclist Chris Boardman, TV writer Russell T Davies and M&S CEO Stuart Rose. It was in the UK's 200 most-streamed songs on Spotify every single day in July 2020. It was also joint second in the official chart of 2021's 'best driving song'. (Oh OK, it was a PR survey for an insurance company.)

The record is the closing track of side three of the Electric Light Orchestra's LP *Out of the Blue*, the one with the spaceship on the cover. The four tracks there are what they call *Concerto for a Rainy Day*, said to explore how the weather affects mood. Nothing it seems affects mood more than *Mr Blue Sky*, though.

A Dutch neuroscientist prostituted his knowledge for Argos's own-brand stereo company Alba and created a formula that worked out what the 'most feel-good song' was. If you're interested in his formula it is *60 + (0.00165 * BPM − 120)2 + (4.376 * Major) + 0.78 * nChords − (Major * nChords)* and the winner (based at least on research of songs already described as 'feel good' by Dutch radio listeners) was of course *Mr Blue Sky* by ELO. If you're interested in what Dr Jacob Jolij said about his formula it is, "I had to cook up a formula. My client had asked me to come up with a formula for PR-purposes. So, how to get from the 'formula' to the list of ultimate feel-good songs? I had little to do with that actually."

Like a stopped clock, these PR maniacs have to be right sometimes, and they also need two fully charged AA batteries shoved in their traps and their knobs twisted until their hands point in the right direction, but there's no denying that *Mr Blue Sky* is incredibly loved. The single sold over four million copies worldwide, which is amazing when you consider that if you just stand around in Brum you will hear it at least once a week for free. How odd, that you can hear a song so often and still find it joyous.

For half of the city it may be because it's played just before the team comes out at St Andrews: so do we love it because we associate it with hope and anticipation? Yes, but watching Birmingham City play football is mostly like fighting a war. It's anticipation for 90-plus minutes of mostly boredom alleviated by terror, hope that the queue for pies at half time won't be too long, or resignation that here comes Jermaine Pennant about to become the first professional footballer in an ankle tag. Yes, it made him relatable to the fans and was a change from most of the team playing like they had a ball and chain, but, still, it's not the bright blue future the song talks about.

Non-blues fans don't hold a grudge about the association, even though Jasper Carrot named his dog after the song. The ELO karaoke night — ELOke "the songs of ELO crucified by drunks" — that we organised at the Sunflower Lounge finished with no audience, everyone on stage *singing Mr Blue Sky* together. It is a song that unites people.

Jeff wrote *Mr Blue Sky* "after locking [himself] away in a Swiss chalet" to write some songs. There was a period of poor weather, and then a nice day: "Everybody knows what I'm talking about," he has said, "it's the thought of 'oh, isn't it nice when the sun comes out'." After listening to and reading many interviews with the Shard End songwriter, his flat Brummie accent sounding like home and his calm self-depreciation charming everyone he talks to, it's clear that Jeff Lynne doesn't really focus too much on what a song's words are about. The chords, the melody, and even most of the recording are done before the lyrics, which he admits to finding hard to write. "It was dark and misty for two weeks, and I didn't come up with a thing," he wrote, "Suddenly the sun shone and it was, 'Wow, look at those beautiful Alps.'" Had it been another shitty day we might have got a song cursing the complete lack of anything to do in Switzerland if it's raining, the joy of a large Toblerone, or the inside of the house's state-mandated nuclear bunker.

In almost every interview Jeff will be asked about how *Mr Blue Sky* came about, and in every one he will say that he had to write some songs for the new double LP. In every one he will be asked about the F to Dm chord progression that the verses 'share' with The Beatles' *Yesterday*, and in every one he will say that "Yeah, it's just a simple melody," and tell us it was a song he wrote with 'posh chords'. In every one he will detail how pretty much everything was in his head before he started to construct the sound, but still praise the work of keyboardist Richard Tandy (it's his voice on the vocoder, the voice of *Mr Blue Sky*) and drummer Bev Bevan (it's him playing the studio's fire extinguisher that makes the clanging sound). Every time we delve deep we find there are no real hidden depths, or if there are they are so hidden that even Jeff doesn't really know where they are. "A lot of people ask me what my songs mean and I have no idea."

I suspect that Jeff has no problem with people making up their own meanings. No-one, including Jeff, knows why in the chorus of *Don't Bring Me Down*, the backing vocalists sing 'Groos'. It was just a placeholder noise. The song was recorded in Germany and 'groos' is close to the German word meaning 'greetings' Jeff left the word in the lyrics. But because it was meaningless, people sang 'Bruce' instead when singing along at gigs. Jeff Lynne just went with it and joined in: he doesn't care what it means. Can you imagine Jimi Hendrix giving up and singing "Excuse me while I kiss this guy"?

Because it means nothing, it can mean anything, and become anything. *Mr Blue Sky* has become a holiday camp 20 miles north of Hull, countless yachts, a pale ale, an eventing horse, a Belgian mattress company, and the high point of the soundtrack of such films as *The Magic Roundabout* (2005), *Guardians of the Galaxy Vol. 2* and *Paul Blart: Mall Cop*.

It soundtracks every promotional video of Birmingham, all of which start with the hazy fog over the Bullring and then move on to a montage of canals and gleaming grade-one office space: and it's still impossible to hate. It even made a choreographed kids dance in Victoria Square — the Commonwealth Games handover ceremony — not embarrassing. There is something Brummie in the hope after adversity.

Birmingham is always changing, going forward, being quietly awful in many ways, but the sun comes out and it can produce beauty like Jeff Lynne produced *Mr Blue Sky*: without being able to explain how it's done. That's why I always play the song at the end of the night, because the night will go away, and it's a reason why Birmingham's not shit and I'll remember it this way.

JB

Please turn me over.

You Have Been Watching

Jon Bounds *(JB)* Jon was voted the '14th Most Influential Person in the West Midlands' in 2008. Subsequently he has not been placed. He's been a football referee, venetian blind maker, cellar man, and a losing Labour council candidate: "No, no chance. A complete no-hoper," said a spoilt ballot. Jon wrote and directed the first ever piece of drama performed on Twitter when he persuaded a cast including MPs and journalists to give over their timelines to perform *Twitpanto*. But all that is behind him. www.popandpolitics.co.uk

Jon Hickman *(JH)* Jon moved to Birmingham from Guernsey in 1997 and still hasn't left. This confuses a lot of people, often including Jon himself. Jon would like to thank everyone for supporting this book which has allowed him to work a lot of this out by thinking out loud. www.theplan.co.uk

Danny Smith *(DS)* Danny has written on culture, pop or otherwise, for Vice, Fused, and Area magazines. He's co-author of Pier Review and a contributor to a smattering of zines, blogs, and other ephemera. He's sold encyclopedias in the Australian outback, taught archery to kids from the ghetto of New Jersey, wrestled with hippies at forgotten festivals, and once met god on the dancefloor of the Que Club in the early 2000s. Danny is currently asleep under a mountain awaiting the people of Britain to need him again. Twitter: @probablydrunk Instagram: @probablydrunk23

Danny and the Jons have worked together on a number of projects over the years. Much of their collaboration has come under the umbrella of Paradise Circus and Birmingham: It's Not Shit which has produced a blog, a stage show and a book, *101 Things Birmingham Gave the World*. Together they make up three quarters of the podcast *Beware of the Leopard* along with another long-term collaborator, Mark Steadman.

In 2011 Jon B and Danny took it upon themselves to visit all fifty two working pleasure piers in the country in two weeks, a journey chronicled in the pun-first, project-later, book *Pier Review*, which was published by Summersdale. It was described (by them) as "On the Road meets On the Buses". They also published the literary magazine without rules Dirty Bristow.

Front cover by Foka Wolf Foka Wolf is, in his words, a "Multi-Award Winning Professional Gobshite". A notorious art vandal beloved by the people of Birmingham for squirting his mind yoghurt all over the walls of the city and beyond. When we asked him to write a bio he told us "write what you want about me". Foka Wolf has six fingers on each hand, smells of the swimming baths, and has a permanent erection he calls 'vlad'.

Thanks To

Thank you to Julia Gilbert, Adam Juniper and Libby Bounds for editorial support and to Mark Steadman for always keeping us in sync.

We're also grateful to those who contributed memories of Snobs for our Big Wednesday. We won't say which are whose as it happened to us all, but thanks to David S, SR, Stephen Lee, Howard Wilkinson, Russell Parker, Claire Spencer, Michelle G, Katie M, Chris, Ms Anonimiss, Marco Palanuto, Vicki, Tin, Jonny G, Jane Trobridge, Fox, Ste Tonks, Jeyklan Hyde, Clare Rawlings, Duran Duran Karen, MF, DJR, Conor, Dave aka Numbdave, Louise Gossage, Helena Barron, Jim, Marek Drzymalski and deviantdoug.

Patrons of the arts

Thank you to everyone who pledged on Kickstarter. Possibly our favourites are Mark Aspinall and Danny Webster who pledged for the Peaky Binder edition. In this we promised to print the book out for them on A4 and pop it in a ring binder, this was more work than we thought, but we're still proud of the pun. Less complicated thanks to:

- Adam 'no nick name' Juniper
- Adam Regan
- Ade Brown
- Alex Shough
- Alex Simpson

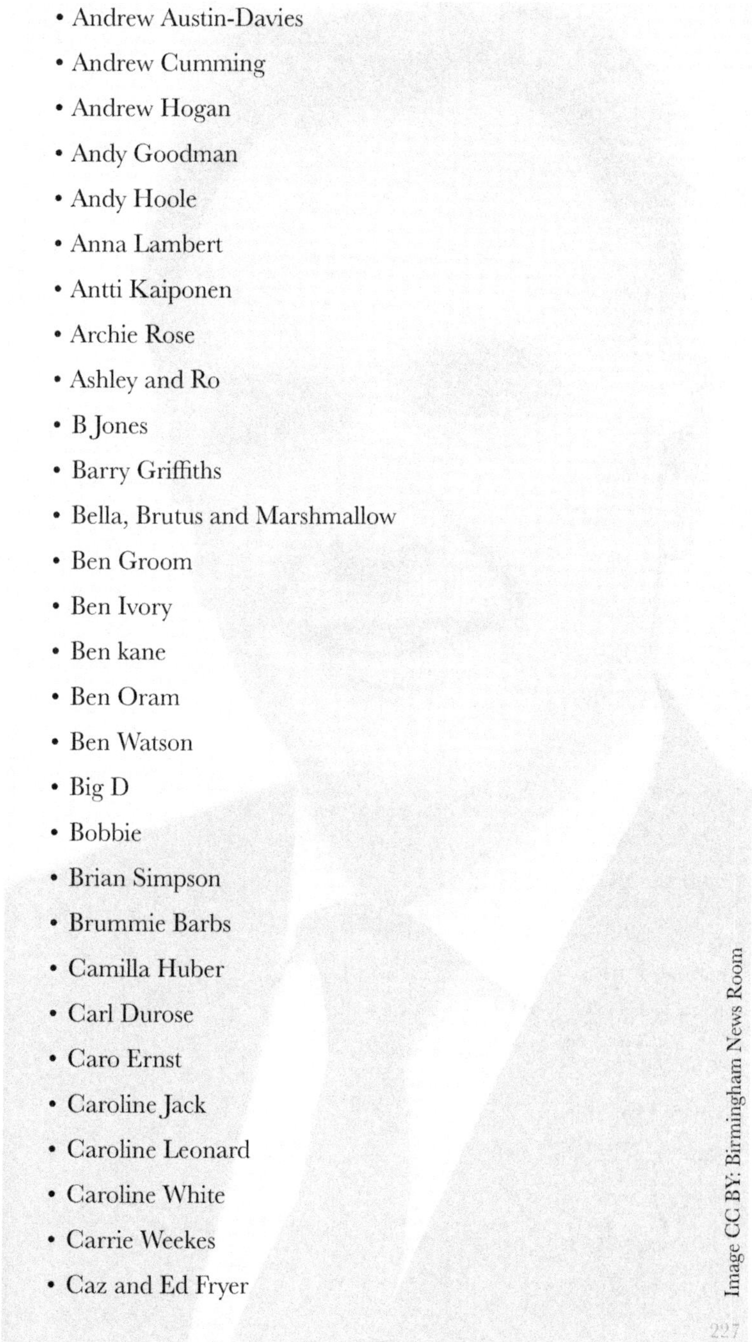

- Andrew Austin-Davies
- Andrew Cumming
- Andrew Hogan
- Andy Goodman
- Andy Hoole
- Anna Lambert
- Antti Kaiponen
- Archie Rose
- Ashley and Ro
- B Jones
- Barry Griffiths
- Bella, Brutus and Marshmallow
- Ben Groom
- Ben Ivory
- Ben kane
- Ben Oram
- Ben Watson
- Big D
- Bobbie
- Brian Simpson
- Brummie Barbs
- Camilla Huber
- Carl Durose
- Caro Ernst
- Caroline Jack
- Caroline Leonard
- Caroline White
- Carrie Weekes
- Caz and Ed Fryer

Image CC BY: Birmingham News Room

- Chris Maher
- Chris Williams
- Christian 'Rusty' Holloway
- Conor Farrell
- Dan Murphy
- Dan Zas
- Daniel Gardner
- Danny Webster
- Darren McKinley
- Dave Ritchie
- David Ault
- David J. Lodwig
- David Nash
- David Rapson
- Deb Ritchie
- Diamondflamer
- Don Lucknow
- Donna and Karli Watson
- Dubber and Michela
- Duncan Ward
- Eddie Thomas
- Emma Barton
- Emma Birch
- Emma Cee
- Emma Daley
- Emma Minshall
- Ernie Becclestone
- Flossie Aylin
- Gareth Saunders

- Gemma Doorne
- George Attwell Gerhards
- George Preston
- Gibbo
- Graeme Rose
- Graham Tierney
- Hannah Culloty
- Hannah Davis
- Harry Vale
- Hayley Dalton
- Helen Rehman
- Hilary Foster
- Himanshu Ojha
- Ian Cook
- Ian Pleace
- Ian Robathan
- Ian Rushbury
- James Vickery
- James Watson
- Jamie Godsall
- Jane Trobridge
- Jem Parry
- Jen B
- Jez Collins
- Jez Higgins
- Jill Arbuckle
- Jo Woodward
- Joe Cartwright
- Joe Fleming

- John Manison
- John McCoy
- John McKeon
- John O'Shea
- John Paul Houghton
- Jonathan Hopkins
- Jonathan Treml
- Jonny Rimmer
- Joseph Costello
- Julia Gilbert
- Julian Coleman
- Kai Lung
- Kate Mascarenhas
- Kathy Jane Hopkin
- Kellie Walton
- Kelly Cobbing
- Keri Davies
- Kevin Fellows
- Kevin Lewis
- KP McKenna
- Lauren Burnard
- Laurence Saunders
- Lee McPherson
- Lee Navin
- Lee-Anne Powell
- Leigh Cotterill
- Lesley Gabriel
- Liam Brooker
- Liz Dexter

- Lucy Chambers
- Lucy Rainsford
- Luke Jerromes
- Lynda Bowen
- Mark Chapman
- Mark Gallagher
- Mark Hill
- Mark Steadman
- Mark Tredgold
- Martin Bailey
- Martin Price
- Mary
- Matt Andrews
- Matt King
- Matthew Alton
- Matthew Cannings
- Matthew Somerville
- Max McLoughlin
- Max Woolf
- Michael Jones
- Michael Stanley
- Michael Whitehouse
- Mike Duff
- Mike Reilly
- Neil W. Law
- Neil Watson
- Nick, Jenny and Cal Drew
- Nicky Getgood
- Olly MacNamee

- Pads
- Paul Hanna
- Paul Scott
- Pavlos Khetab
- Philip Lancaster
- Rakie Bennett
- Richard Harrison
- Richard Phipps
- Rob Blake
- Rob Walsh
- Rob Wickings
- Robert Shaw
- Rose Poulter
- Russ L
- Ryan Parish
- RyeDawg
- Sam Kennedy
- Sam Launchbury
- Sasha K
- Scott Adcock
- Sean Higgins
- Shivaji Shiva
- Siân Morgan
- Simon Best
- Simon Dixon
- Simon Laws
- Simon Mills
- Simon Myring

- Simon Stokes
- Stephan Work
- Stephen Cooper / Kebablog
- Stephen Morris
- Stephen Parkes
- Steve Nicholls
- Steve Tanner
- Steven D Quirke
- Stuart Griffiths
- Stuart Harrison
- The Smalley family
- The Snowleys
- theaardvark
- Tim Ellis
- Tim Mobbs
- Toby Draper
- Tom Campbell
- Tom Lennon
- Tony Hackett
- Tristan Beer
- Trudie Bagwell
- William Hill, Ex-Brummie
- YeltzDoc

Not bored yet? For more photos of Sir Albert Bore join the The Same Photo Of Albert Bore Every Day Facebook Group

Also from Paradise Circus

101 Things Birmingham Gave the World

This is the book that proves that Birmingham is not just the crucible of the Industrial Revolution, but the cradle of civilisation. From the team behind hit Birmingham miscellany, Paradise Circus, comes the definitive guide to the 101 things that made the world what it is today — and all of them were made in Birmingham. Read how Birmingham gave the world the wonders of tennis, nuclear war, the Beatles, 'that smell of eggs' and many more… 97 more.

"*101 Things Birmingham Gave The World*, is not a Birmingham of the memory. It is a living breathing thing, wrestling with the city's contradictions, press-ganging the typically arch and understated humour of the Brummie, and an army of little-known facts, both trivial and monumental, into reshaping its confusing reputation." **Stewart Lee**

"Clearly a book for people with an immature sense of humour" **Sam12345**

"The industrial language in some items was uncalled for" **Ms. J. A. Russell**

280 Stops

Next time you're on the bus look around you: everyone has a story, everyone is going somewhere, everyone is thinking something. They're the lead actors in their own drama, and everyone around them is the supporting cast. Including you.

Now meet 11 people who rode the 11 bus on the 11th November, 2009 and step into their shoes, hear their stories, and see all of the connections between these strangers.

280 Stops is a tribute to two wonderful things: the 11 bus route which runs through Birmingham (oh, and bits of Solihull and Sandwell), and Geoff Ryman's novel/website 253.

This page contains Andy Street's action on homelessness

Printed in Great Britain
by Amazon